LADS
A GUIDE TO **RESPECT** AND **CONSENT**

ALAN BISSETT

LADS

A GUIDE TO RESPECT AND CONSENT

STEP UP, SPEAK OUT AND CREATE POSITIVE CHANGE

wren & rook

First published in Great Britain in 2023 by Wren & Rook

Text copyright © Alan Bissett 2023
All rights reserved.

The right of Alan Bissett to be identified as the author of
this Work has been asserted by them in accordance with
the Copyright, Designs & Patents Act 1988.

ISBN: 978 1 5263 6502 6

10 9 8 7 6 5 4 3 2 1

Wren & Rook
An imprint of
Hachette Children's Group
Part of Hodder & Stoughton
Carmelite House
50 Victoria Embankment
London EC4Y 0DZ

An Hachette UK Company
www.hachette.co.uk
www.hachettechildrens.co.uk

Printed and bound in Great Britain by
Clays Ltd, Elcograf S.p.A.

The website addresses (URLs) included in this book were valid at
the time of going to press. However, it is possible that contents or
addresses may have changed since the publication of this book.
No responsibility for any such changes can be accepted by either
the author or the publisher.

This book has been reviewed by an expert who runs gender equality
training with young men, and an educational psychologist.

This book is dedicated to my sons,

Fergus and Ivor

Good lads

CONTENTS

Introduction 9

Chapter 1
Flirting, with Disaster 37

Chapter 2
Porn on the Rocks 63

Chapter 3
Locker Room Talk 83

Chapter 4
The 'Nice' Guys 109

Chapter 5
The Worst Guys 125

Chapter 6
The Good Guys 167

Resources 190

References 194

Acknowledgements 198

Biography 200

INTRODUCTION

When you think of a 'lad' what do you picture?

A young guy, out with his mates, looking for excitement? A guy with a bit of bravado and swagger? One of the gang? One of the *lads*. A good guy? An arrogant guy? A funny guy?

Well, you'd better have a think about it, because your house is about to be full of lads.

There's a party round at yours! Your parents are away. I hope you've tidied, cos the place was covered in pizza boxes this morning, and also there are girls coming, who you hope to impress. **You want this to be the party people talk about for months, for all the right reasons.**

The party's in full swing! You wander through from the kitchen into the living room – what do you want to see?

Everyone's chilled. Girls and boys are chatting to each other, interested in each other's conversation. There is smiling and laughing. Some people are even dancing, enjoying the music. The hours you put into making that playlist have paid off. People are having a good time.

Duuuude!
Nailed it!

You can relax.

Or else you could walk into this: there are fewer people in the room than before, because somebody's brought along **THAT GUY**. He's drunk and making inappropriate comments, cracking edgy jokes that only he thinks are funny, grinding against the girls who are dancing. **You can feel the tension in the room, right?** The girls are unhappy about it. Probably some of the boys are unhappy about it. But no one is saying anything about it, because the whole situation is a bit **intimidating** and **awkward**.

Maybe **THAT GUY** doesn't think he's being a problem. Maybe he even thinks he's *just being a lad*.

I mean, c'mon, it's a laugh!
It's a party, lighten up!

Those girls got dressed like that so guys would look at them and would give them compliments. What girl doesn't want to hear that her chest looks great in that dress and would look even better out of it?

(EESH! FOR THE RECORD, NO GIRL WANTS TO HEAR THIS.)

So, the question for you is: **what kind of vibe are you trying to create at this party?** Everyone apart from **THAT GUY** seemed to be enjoying the first one a lot more.

***

Now, imagine that party is the whole world, and there's not just one of **THAT GUY**.

THERE ARE
MILLIONS
OF THEM.

That might seem like a grim thought, but the truth is there *are* millions of them, **and they're everywhere.** Because if we're being honest – and if nothing else, this must be an honest conversation – almost every guy I know has been ***THAT GUY*** at some point. I'm not saying they've done those *specific* things, and for some the thought of even offending a girl might mortify them. But whether they intended to or not, they will have, as we say in Scotland,

ACTED THE GOAT.[1]

It's not to say that in all sorts of situations men aren't heroic or noble or kind or charismatic or loving or witty. We can quote from movies, sink a mean pool ball and put our hands in the air with everyone else for the chorus. But to some woman, somewhere, we probably have been, or will be, ***THAT GUY.***

THIS BOOK IS ABOUT HOW TO AVOID BEING

➡ *THAT GUY.* ⬅

---

[1] Means 'being too boisterous or over-confident'.

BECAUSE, MATE, HE'S A BIG PROBLEM.

***

In 2021, I was one of the team who worked on a short video commissioned by Police Scotland called

It featured a series of young men talking to camera, each of them asking the audience a different question:

---

[2] To give proper credit, the video was conceived and produced by Stand Design Agency and filmed by Forest of Black, both Glasgow-based, on behalf of Police Scotland. I was commissioned by Stand to help them edit their script.

> Ever called a girl 'doll'
>   or whistled at her walking down the street?
> Ever stared at a woman on the bus
>   or said to your mate, 'I'd do that'?
> Ever given a girl a compliment, like 'Nice . . .'[3]
>   and wondered why you didn't get a
>   'Thank you'?
>
> Ever slid into a girl's DMs
>   then went ahead and just showed her it?
> Ever bought a lassie dinner
>   and felt that meant she owed you something?
> Ever got her three shots in a row,
>   hoping you'd get a shot of her?
> Then what?
>   Bundled her, wasted, into a taxi and
>   took her back to yours?
> Ever guilt-tripped her?
>   Or pressured her?
>   Or pushed her into it,
>   then left feeling
>   like a lad?
>
> Most men don't look in the mirror and see a problem.
>   But it's staring us right in the face.
>
> Sexual violence starts long before you think it does.
>
> ## Don't be That Guy.

---

[3] This line was actually written as 'Nice arse'. I'm not sure why this was taken out in the video edit. Maybe so they could show it in schools.

During our work on the script, the other two male writers and I discussed some of the behaviour like this that we'd seen. **We shared our own experiences** of being younger and laughing at sexist comments, and we picked apart the masculine culture that we'd all grown up in. We already knew from our conversations with women that they **constantly have to be on their guard for dangerous men**, but we tried to imagine what that must really be like.

It was a bit of downer. But we aren't the ones who have to, y'know, live it.

Much to my surprise, the video spread quickly across the globe, racking up over **200,000 views on YouTube, and getting over 32,000 Retweets and 55,000 Likes on Twitter** at the time, as well as receiving international press and broadcast news coverage, sparking discussion about where the blame for sexual assault truly lies. It meant less talk about women having too much to drink on a night out and more about **men who can't control their behaviour around them.** *Don't Be That Guy* aimed to look at the everyday actions of men who are hoping to get pretty much only one thing out of women, which results in aggressive attitudes towards them becoming normalised.

HEAVY, RIGHT? I KNOW.

But bear with me.

The video struck a nerve because the conversation on girls' and women's safety changed in 2017, as revelations about the Hollywood mogul and serial rapist Harvey Weinstein emerged. **Here was one of the most wealthy and powerful men in Hollywood, who used his status to abuse women and cover up his crimes.** This discussion deepened in the UK during 2021, after the murder of Sarah Everard by a serving police officer, Wayne Couzens, who deceived Everard with a phony arrest over COVID regulations. **The ugly truth,** however, is that there have been countless women like Everard, both before and since, who have died in such a tragic way.

In short, there is a very good reason why so many girls and women of all ages make sure their female friends message them to say they're home safely.

I mean, don't get me wrong, my mum always waited up for me getting in **(thanks, Mum!)**, but I certainly didn't have male pals getting in touch after a night out to check that I was tucked up cosily in my bed. And perhaps boys and men should do this for each other. It is still possible for us to be vulnerable, especially if alcohol is being consumed.

For girls, checking in on each other can be vital.

That's also why back in 2006 a woman called Tarana Burke started the **Me Too movement**, encouraging other women to stand up against this climate of fear. And it's why **#MeToo** went viral on social media around the time of the Weinstein case, as women all over the globe shared their tales of being bullied by, assaulted by or afraid of men.

OK, OK, you're probably thinking: **why am I getting on to you about this?** You would never be violent to a woman! That's good, mate. I'm glad.

YOU'RE ON THE RIGHT TRACK!

But let's talk anyway.

I know this is all stuff no guy really wants to hear – I mean, I don't particularly want to write about it – and this early in the book it's probably a bit off-putting. Maybe you've picked it up and are randomly flicking through the pages in a bookshop, or you've clicked on the preview in Amazon, attracted by the word **LADS** in huge letters on the front (**'I'm a lad! That's me!'**). Possibly your feminist mum has bought this for you, cos, y'know **(finger-wagging)**, 'I think there are a few things you could learn from this, son.' And now you're making a big show of reading it in front of her because you don't want to let her down, but gaaaaawd, even the introduction is a drag.

I get it. None of us wants to look at this issue, especially when terms like **'problematic behaviour'**, **'toxic masculinity'**, **'be better'** and **'patriarchy'** get thrown around like accusations

WHEN YOU HAVEN'T EVEN DONE ANYTHING WRONG! GOD, EXCUSE ME FOR BEING MALE!

Maybe you're even here to take this book down?

And that's fine. Criticism is fine. I understand that this all sounds a bit preachy **(already!)**, and I don't have a leg to stand on anyway, given that I now look back on some of the things I've said to women in the past, and the ways I've acted towards them, and absolutely cringe.

But the truth is, women have been talking about these issues for a very long time and we need to speak about them too. It's not because we're all awful and need to stand there while women queue up to shout at us for it, but because men are *not* awful **(most, anyway)** and can actually make a difference.

So, stick with me, cos by the end of it we're all going to be part of a **BLOODY GREAT, IMPORTANT AND POWERFUL SHIFT**, like in *Endgame*, when the Avengers went back in time and – *spoiler alert* – undid Thanos's snap from *Infinity War*.

Think of ***THAT GUY*** as Thanos.

Yeah, that works.

First off, let me say it: I like being male. I enjoy it. I love the company of other men and I like talking about traditional 'guy stuff' with them: action movies, rock music, big splashy nights out we've been on and famous women we find attractive. That's not *all* we talk about, obviously, but, y'know, that's definitely some of it. **AND IT'S FUN.**

Besides, men make up half of the world's population, and for obvious reasons the species would die out without us.

But we need to have a conversation, man to man, about some of the behaviours that guys often believe to be normal – *expected*, even – **but which have the knock-on effect of making women feel uncomfortable, tense or afraid for their own safety**. This book is about the *kind* of men we are often presumed to be by other men, who want us to validate or mimic their own toxic behaviour – all of which turns out to be bad news for women.

Also, I have two young sons, so I have a vested interest in making sure that they don't become men whom girls and women are anxious about being around. I would feel I'd let them down as a father if I failed in that task, and **also their mum would be very, very disappointed.**

I WANT HER TO BE PROUD OF THEM TOO.

***

Let me give you an example from my past of my utter cluelessness with girls, which now makes me fold like a deckchair with embarrassment. The year is 1994 and I'm eighteen years old. Blur's *Parklife* and Oasis's *Definitely Maybe* are riding high in the charts. Posters for Quentin Tarantino's *Pulp Fiction* adorn every student hall of residence in the land. I'm at the student union bar of my university and, **as we all know, there is literally no hornier creature in the land than an eighteen-year-old boy**. I'm chatting to this girl I fancy, and as the night draws to a close, I realise I will probably have to make my move. Before I can do so, however, she announces that she needs to go to the ladies' toilets, and as she goes in, she stumbles.

So I wait for her.

Outside the ladies' toilets.

After a while, she comes out, looking a bit worse for wear, being held up by her friend. **'Don't worry,'** her friend tells her, **'I'm sure the creepy guy is away now.'** I look around for the creepy guy she's talking about. Her friend notices me and shoots me a look that seems to say: *don't even try . . .*

Wait. The creepy guy is me?
What have I done to deserve that?

I WALK BACK TO MY STUDENT HALLS, CONFUSED AND ANGRY.

OH WHAT, I'M NOT ALLOWED TO CHAT SOMEONE UP NOW?

I'M NOT ALLOWED TO FANCY A GIRL?

URGH, FEMINISTS!

It's only much later, with a few more years under my belt, that I'm able to see things from the female point of view, and **suddenly the picture shifts.**

Her friend has been watching me attach myself to this girl for most of the night in the hope of getting somewhere. **She's seen her get progressively more drunk.** She's seen her go to the bathroom (where women often go to try to escape men who won't leave them alone) and has gone to check in with her. The girl has possibly said something like, **'I can't get rid of this guy,'** and her friend has promised to get her home safely, even if it means propping her up to do so. Then she's come out of the bathroom to find me waiting there.

Like, y'know, a creep.

This picture only became clear once I saw it through their eyes. The world tilted on its axis and my skin turned crimson. I learned some valuable lessons: **don't try to hit on drunk girls. Don't hang around them all night. Certainly don't wait outside the bathroom for them.**

Turns out, they don't like it.

Perhaps you've never made that mistake, but chances are that a lot of boys have done something of that nature, something they'd thought was innocuous – something they thought she'd maybe even *like* – but instead made a girl's skin crawl. And the reason I was able to learn from that incident, as opposed to writing both girls off as uptight killjoys, was through the act of trying to see men as women see us.

Now, I'm not trying to position myself as some sensitive gentleman of the world and you as a backwards cave troll who needs educating from the likes of me, because **I continued to make mistakes over the years and probably will again,** even if I'm not hanging around outside the ladies' loo like a total weirdo any more. But I am pointing out that the best way to understand why a situation went wrong is to surrender our defensiveness, step outside ourselves and look at it from a different angle.

Men are not often encouraged to look at things from the female angle. And this failure costs women dearly.

***

OK, no more messing about. **Here's the difficult bit.** Let's get it dealt with early. There won't be any jokes in this section, I'm afraid. By the end of the book, after some grim moments, you will be able to mentally kick back on the beach, drinking from a coconut shell. First, however, let's do the work . . .

If you ask most women whether they've ever experienced a man making them feel afraid, you're probably going to get 100% of them saying yes. That's not an official statistic, but the ones on the next page are:

According to Rape Crisis England & Wales, nine out ten girls of school age say that sexist name-calling or being sent unwanted 'dick pics' happens to either them or other girls their age.

UN Women (a United Nations entity dedicated to female empowerment) report that 86% of women aged eighteen to twenty-four have experienced sexual harassment in public.

Globally, an estimated 736 million women – almost one in three – have been subjected to physical or sexual violence by a man.

In any given year, one in every thirty women is raped or sexually assaulted, which means it's likely at least one woman you know has experienced this in the last twelve months.

Not looking good out there, is it?

This isn't to say that rape doesn't happen to men. Unfortunately, it does, though it is nearly always done to men by men, almost never by women.

It's not to say either that women aren't capable of being violent towards their partners, and men who experience this should not be belittled or sidelined. **Help should be available for them too.**

It's undeniably the case, however, that the scale of sexual violence against women by men utterly dwarfs these other problems. Comparing them would be like comparing the size of the sun and the moon but saying they're 'the same' because they're both celestial objects.

Men often like to tell themselves this behaviour erupts from random lunatics like Wayne Couzens, Jimmy Savile or Ted Bundy (by all means look them up online, but beware, it's grim). While it's true that these are the very worst examples of the problem – **men utterly devoid of empathy for women and full only of hatred for them** – they are also, in some ways, a distraction.

The statistics quoted on the previous page cannot be accounted for by 'random lunatics' alone.

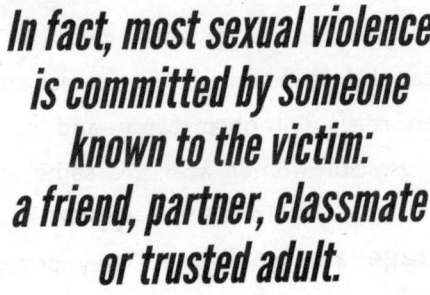

> In fact, most sexual violence is committed by someone known to the victim: a friend, partner, classmate or trusted adult.

It emerges from a culture in which females are viewed as sexual objects, there for use by men, regardless of how women might feel about the matter. It emerges out of a society in which women's worries about their own safety are not taken seriously.

It's what we were trying to get across with the **DON'T BE THAT GUY** video. Actions that might seem trivial to whoever's doing them – staring at a girl, wolf-whistling or cat-calling – can escalate to more serious ones, **such as sending unwanted dick pics, trying to get her drunk to take advantage of her and even assault.** It's a sliding scale of behaviour, to be sure, but it all starts by disrespecting women's boundaries.

Man, I'm dying to get back to cracking jokes, but we're not *quite* there yet.

It all begins in the way we guys think about girls and women in the first place. We often have this idea that women are strange, exotic, almost alien creatures, eternally unknowable, impossible to read, full of mystery and fundamentally different to us. But women feel the same spectrum of emotions that we do, from **love, happiness and hope to spite, rage and jealousy**. They poop, burp and fart, the same as we do, and they can't find a pair of matching socks in the morning either. Women are, first and foremost, *human beings*. **Just like men.** This really shouldn't need saying, but believe me, some men do forget it.

This is a book about getting comfortable in calling out the bad behaviour that stems from this mindset.

It's about accepting that although you're not to blame for men's actions in the past, you do have the power to create positive change in the future.

And it's a book that will help you feel confident about navigating the modern minefield of relationships and interacting with girls, while also being someone who makes them feel safe, heard and respected.

Because *that's* the guy everyone needs right now.[4]

Not That Guy.

[4] Superhero 'call to arms' music right here.

Don't get me wrong, you should want to do the right thing *anyway*, as it's a good feeling and it makes the world a better place to live in, but following this path will also (whisper it!) make you that bit more attractive to girls. Your relationships with them will improve. **And this will make you, and them, much happier all round.**

Previous generations of men, drenched in Old Spice aftershave[5] and sinking pints of bitter at the bar, moaning about their wives, got so much of this wrong.

YOURS IS THE GENERATION THAT CAN MAKE IT RIGHT.

The fact that you are even reading this book and have persevered this far – instead of chucking it against the wall and going, **'Oh, for god's sake!'** – is a great start. You should honestly be proud of yourself for that, and if you get to the end of it, you should be even prouder.

If you can do that, then you're not really the problem.

It's not a long book, and you can have as many toilet breaks as you like.

---

[5] Ask your grandad.

I promise not to be waiting outside for you to come out.

(And if that made you shudder, think how she felt!)

A note first about who this book is for. I'm writing this because it's what **I wish I had known as a boy.** But I'm aware that not every boy reading it will be the same as I was.

I am a white Scottish man who grew up working class but is university educated. I'm probably about 85% straight. I'm not gay enough to call myself bisexual but there are still some men I find huuuuugely attractive.

Among those of you reading this, there will be a variety of identities. **This book has been written with boys in mind, but this is still a broad group of people.** You may be a person of colour, or middle class, or English or Irish or Welsh or American or Australian (or if I'm lucky enough that this book reaches translation, French, Norwegian, Indian or Mexican), or a combination of many of these things, and more besides.

You might not even be male at all. Perhaps you're a woman or girl, notebook and pen poised, curious about whether or not I'm going to arse this all up. I hope I don't. My wish is for you to reach the end of this book with a sense of optimism that things will change.

My point is that your background and identity inform your experiences, your take on things and your probable reaction to this book.

Most of the behaviour I'm going to write about is carried out by heterosexual boys and men. I'm interested in the way that we act around each other and towards women, and I want to dig deeper into that. But I'd still invite those of you who don't identify in this way to keep on learning. There may be some of you out there still wrestling with your sexuality. Take your time. **It's not a race and some of us never reach a definitive answer.**

There's space for everyone, after all.

If you are a member of the LGBTQ+ community, there's room for you to play a role here as confidants and allies to women – **calling out bad behaviour when it is safe to do so** – and as friends to straight men, because no one wants their mate to be acting the total fool. These are also human issues at play here, and **the overall message of this book is about consent and respect: respecting boundaries, respecting others and respecting yourself.** We can all learn a thing or two, no matter who you fancy or who you are in a relationship with.

This book is also partly a self-reflection – sifting through my own memories, observations and shortcomings – and so is written mainly for people with a similar sexuality and relationship to women as my own. Because of this, my experiences may not always be representative of others', but my hope is that there is still something worthwhile for everyone to take away from this book.

So if you are a guy who is attracted to girls, it's important for me to reassure you. Look, you're growing up, you're still probably naive about a lot of things (I know I was!) and your emotions are a riot of low self-esteem and excitement.

Of course you're going to make mistakes.

Everyone can forgive that, if your intentions are true. You hold your hands up and try to make amends for any harm done, or at least learn from it. I'm guessing you're probably a good guy who just wants to have a better relationship with girls. If that's true, then don't worry, this isn't going to be too hard on you.

After all, as Depeche Mode once sang, people are people.

We just need to make sure we also apply that view to women.

***

OK, first off, how do we talk to them? There she is, standing at the other side of your house party, nodding along to your playlist. She might even be part of the reason you threw this party in the first place, hoping she'd come.

What are you going to say? Argh!

Done your hair? Put on your dancing shoes? Chewed a breath mint?

OK, WE'RE GOING IN...

CHAPTER 1
FLIRTING, WITH DISASTER

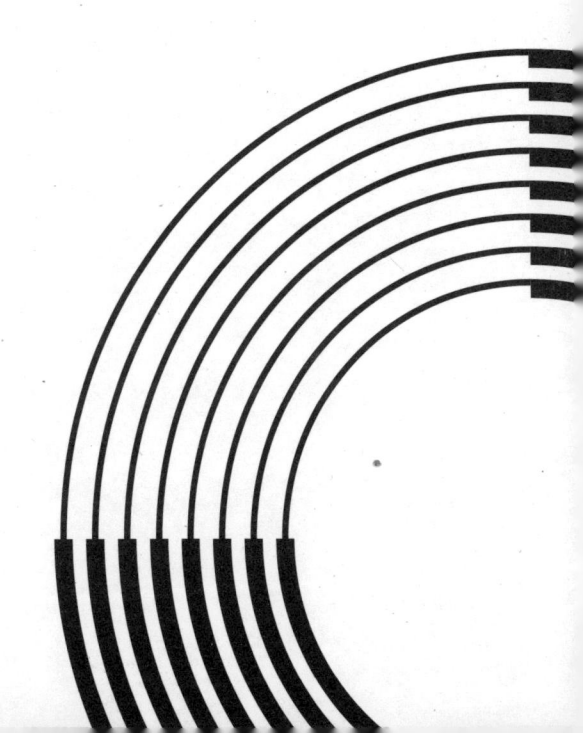

We're going to start by looking at the most common terrain that men must traverse when it comes to relations with women.

Yup, it's that awkward, necessary, indefinable thing:

FLIRTING.

As almost every man's experience will tell you, it can all so very easily go wrong with flirting – very, very wrong – when all we want is that party where everyone's **cool, happy and relaxed**.

Flirting is a great thing. In fact, it is vital to the future of the human race. **Flirting done well is consensual, playful and exciting** – the ultimate dopamine hit that offers the possibility of more . . . or not.

But flirting *badly* – making the wrong moves or saying the wrong things – is the first sign to a woman that a man is not quite **trustworthy** or at least might lack what it takes to connect with her.

I understand, of course, that for most boys, talking to girls, especially ones they fancy, is an absolute minefield. Some will find it harder than others to navigate social situations and their unwritten rules. I remember nothing more intense than the roiling mix of attraction to a girl and terror at approaching her. And back then there was no social media, online dating or WhatsApp, so it all had to be done **face to face or over the phone.**

So cringe.

But there are some basic things that guys can do in conversation which, while not exactly guaranteeing that she'll fall at your feet, will at least up the chances of her liking you.

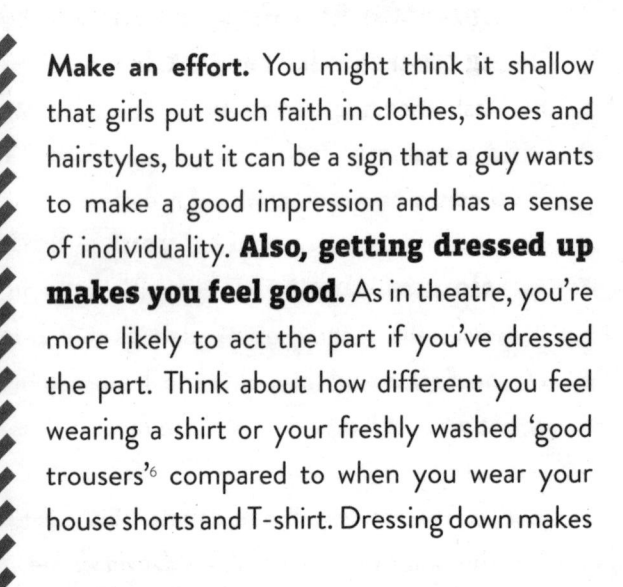

Make an effort. You might think it shallow that girls put such faith in clothes, shoes and hairstyles, but it can be a sign that a guy wants to make a good impression and has a sense of individuality. **Also, getting dressed up makes you feel good.** As in theatre, you're more likely to act the part if you've dressed the part. Think about how different you feel wearing a shirt or your freshly washed 'good trousers'[6] compared to when you wear your house shorts and T-shirt. Dressing down makes

---

[6] Scots is such a rich language that we have not one but three words for trousers: 'troosers', 'trews' and 'breeks'. If I'd written 'guid breeks', you wouldn't have had a clue what I was saying, but just try saying it in a Scottish accent for fun anyway.

you feel down. Dressing up makes you feel, well, up. All you need is something that helps you stand out – a cool picture on your T-shirt, a pattern on your collar, an interesting belt – something unusual and eye-catching that shows you have a personality and *some* sense of style. You don't have to go overboard and wear, like, a hat with feathers on it. That's not to say you couldn't rock a hat with feathers on it, of course. **You just *don't* have *to*.**

Be gracious. Most girls – most *people*, in fact – **appreciate kindness, manners and being treated with respect**. It may sound old-fashioned but it's true.

Find common ground. It's a lot easier to talk to someone about **a thing you're both passionate about**, whether it's a band, a movie, a TV show or a video game. One of the first things my wife and I ever spoke about when we first met was the fact that she preferred 1980s David Bowie to 1970s David Bowie. We had a fun wee debate about that, but the point was: *we both liked David Bowie.*

Oh, and don't mock her taste in things. Nobody enjoys that. She enjoys what she enjoys. So do you.[7]

Ask her questions. People like to talk about their own lives. Women can often feel as though men don't really listen to them and only want to talk about themselves. Turn that around. Show that you're **the sort of person who cares about who she is**, what she likes doing and what her opinions on things are.

Tell interesting stories. People love a good storyteller, but a good story doesn't go on *too* long and also has a point. Stories that ramble on and then just peter out are a waste of everyone's time. Stories that have an interesting twist that makes everyone go, **'Ooooh'**, on the other hand, are what people want to hear. Also: avoid dark stories. She probably doesn't want to know that a guy you used to pal about with is now, unfortunately, in jail for murdering his neighbour. She maybe does want to know that you rode a horse on holiday once, though?

---

[7] That said, seventies David Bowie IS better than eighties David Bowie. Despite *Labyrinth* and *Let's Dance*.

Well, who knows, maybe she likes true crime more than horses. I just wouldn't take the chance.

Use humour. Who doesn't enjoy a good laugh? **Who doesn't like folk who make them laugh?** But don't tell dirty jokes, jokes at her expense or jokes about other people. They just make someone seem coarse or cruel.

Be self-deprecating. Showing that you can laugh at yourself proves that you are confident and self-assured. We are all ridiculous humans. **Embrace that.**

Bring others up. Talk positively about people. I mean, that's a general rule for life anyway, but it might be especially important to her and to friends of hers. It shows you are an upbeat and generous person and means she's more likely to feel you'll fit in with her group. **Never a bad thing.** Conversely, if you're always moaning about other folk . . .

Well, do you like moaners? ***Exactly.***

Presuming all is going well so far, the crunch then comes: asking her out. **If she says yes?**

SCORE!

I hope you have a wonderful date.

But what if she says no? You know what that means. You're ugly. You're weird. You're not good enough for her. What possibly made you think you *were*? **Get back under your bridge, troll!**

Obviously I'm joking, but that *is* how rejection feels. It's the worst feeling in the world, right?

Well, it all depends on how you look at it. You can train yourself out of taking it as a bullet to your self-esteem by reminding yourself that it's just a matter of what she wants not matching with what you want. After all, you've rejected other people too, and will probably do so again if you feel that you don't connect.

You have that right.
So does she.

By far the best thing you can do is accept the rejection, maybe feel a little deflated for a bit, and then move on. Just know that we've all felt it. **No one is superhuman.** Ryan Reynolds, Chris Evans, Michael B. Jordan, Tom Hardy, Henry Cavill, Jack Grealish[8] – every single one of them will have been rejected by women at some point in their life and will probably have been heartbroken about it. **Mate, welcome to the great chain of life that links us all together in pain.**

But sometimes our understandably negative feelings about being turned down can lead to unhealthy patterns: seeing it as a 'challenge' and stepping up the chase; avoiding women altogether and thinking of them as people who can only hurt you; or engaging them aggressively, 'negging' them or being cruel.

Negging, by the way, means giving a girl a subtle comment designed to undermine her confidence, such as,

> **'That's an interesting dress, I've seen three girls wearing it tonight.'**

It's a mean-spirited tactic, and **a Red Flag**.

---

[8] Insert your own Attractive Man here.

What's a Red Flag? Well, that's a sign that a man might be something more than he appears to be, something unpleasant, and, guys, we raise these Red Flags all the time without even knowing we're doing it. Here are three Red Flags that we often raise when we try to (in my favourite old-style term for the practice) 'woo'.

>>>>>>>>>>>>>>>>>>>>>>>>>>>>>>>

1. OVER-COMPLIMENTING

Wait, what? Girls love compliments, right? That's why they spend hours in front of the mirror? I mean, **who doesn't want to be told they look good**?

It's true. They might want to be told they look good. Don't we all, sometimes? But there's a time and a place and a way to do it, so that it feels genuine and kind, instead of suggesting that you're trying to picture what she looks like naked.

Things a woman won't enjoy a man she doesn't know complimenting her on:

- ✘ Her legs
- ✘ Her hips
- ✘ Her bust
- ✘ Her rear
- ✘ Her feet
- ✘ Her scent
- ✘ Her eyes
- ✘ Her smile

Her eyes and smile? OK, so those last two might seem innocent enough, and if the girl already knows and likes you, then telling her she has a beautiful smile can be really sweet. **But it's all about context**. No woman wants a random stranger on the train or in the street telling her she has lovely eyes or asking her to smile.

IT'S CREEPY.

As for her legs, hips, bust and bum? I'd steer clear of talking about them entirely. Well, that's unless you are already in a trusting and intimate relationship with her.

Otherwise, noooooo.

And why would you even mention her feet, dude?

Get it right and a heartfelt compliment can be a lovely moment, making someone feel good about themselves. But get it wrong and it will sound like you're perving on her. Things a woman generally will enjoy men complimenting her on:

- ✔ Her style
- ✔ Her jewellery
- ✔ Her intelligence
- ✔ Her humour
- ✔ Her achievements

These are the things that make her a person, not an object. But even then, don't overdo it, otherwise it will feel a bit forced, desperate and clingy.

I remember a female friend of mine telling me that her date just wouldn't stop praising her. It had started with her hair, then moved on to her eyes and her smile, until eventually he'd said, 'And you have lovely earlobes.'

'Earlobes?' she'd replied, confused.

She'd begun the date fancying him, but the weight of his compliments – and about her *earlobes*, of all things – ended up feeling *a bit too much*.

Forced. Desperate. Clingy . . .

Still feel confused? The basic rule is:

BE GENUINE.

If you know a girl well and think she likes you, it's OK to give her certain compliments. Perhaps you really admire that she's brilliant at sport or think she's massively clever. Maybe she has a really unique dress sense or great taste in music. It's nice to tell her so, and she'll be flattered. But don't go over the top with an obvious ulterior motive, hoping your gushing might win her attention. **That's when it stops feeling genuine.**

And steer clear of talking about her earlobes.

I mean, who has nice earlobes anyway?

>>>>>>>>>>>>>>>>>>>>>>>>>>

2. WEARING HER DOWN

Romantic comedies have a lot to answer for here. Yep, it's the **'if at first you don't succeed' approach**!

Implied in it is the idea that a woman just doesn't fancy you *yet*.

Think about the number of movies or TV plots you've seen in which the following happens: guy meets girl. Guy and girl do not get on. Guy and girl bicker. **AND YET!** Is there a spark between them? Something unsaid? A friendship begins – or is it more? – thwarted when either the man or the woman learns that the target of their affections is with someone else. Never fear, he or she will soon realise the error of their ways once they see who has been standing in front of them all along: our hero/heroine. The message is: just keep at it long enough for them to wake up to your true, inner beauty.

WEAR HER DOWN.

In real life, the Wear Her Down approach is utterly exhausting for women (and surely also for men). She thought she was making herself clear. She isn't with you *for a reason*. Trying to 'wear her down' suggests that you think she doesn't really know her own mind, that you know it better than she does, and that every time she turns around you are going to be there.

That's not as reassuring as you might think it is.

Sometimes the Wear Her Down tactic can take a sinister turn. A good example is the character of John Bender, played by Judd Nelson, in 1985's *The Breakfast Club*, widely regarded as **the best teen movie ever made**. Over the course of the film, Bender, a kid from the rough side of the tracks, bullies, mocks, negs and even gropes the character of Claire Standish, played by Molly Ringwald, the rich, spoilt, popular girl. He wages this campaign to destroy her confidence in full view of their classmates, to the point where she breaks down in tears.

HE'S AWFUL.

Yet there she is at the end of the film, swooning into his arms.

What's the message? ***WEAR HER DOWN.***

It's maybe no coincidence that *The Breakfast Club* was written and directed by a man.

In real life, if you try this approach, girls will not be swooning into your arms. **They will hate you.**

A girl should believe that you want the best for her. It is intoxicating to feel liberated by someone, to know that you can be truly yourself around them, rather than being forced into the straitjacket of what someone else wants you to be.

If it's not working out, if it's clear that you're not making her happy, **accept that and move on.**

As the saying goes: if you love someone, set them free.

>>>>>>>>>>>>>>>>>>>>>>>>>>>>>

3. THE GRAND GESTURE

Romantic comedies have a lot to answer for here too.

In tandem with Wearing Her Down, the theory seems to go: if I can demonstrate just *how* much I'm prepared to do for her, the lengths to which I'll go to win her, surely that's worth something? It's a scaled-up version of the attitude that if you've bought her an ice-cream or paid for her cinema tickets, then that must mean you're owed at least a kiss. **(You're not, by the way – we'll come to this later.)** It then stops becoming generosity and starts becoming a transaction, and what girl wants to feel like you're paying her to give you 'something extra'?

The Grand Gesture takes that attitude and ruuuuuuuns with it.

Grand Gestures from films and TV that would never work

in real life – some of which would get you locked up in jail, and all of which would mean people looking at you funny – include:

Sprinting past airport security to reach her.
(Love Actually)

Buying a ticket for her flight to propose to her on the plane.
(Crazy Rich Asians)

Interrupting someone's live performance and forcing everyone in the room to watch her dance.
(Dirty Dancing)

Interrupting a graduation speech and proclaiming love for her.
(Crazy Stupid Love)

Turning up on the red carpet at an awards show in front of the world's media and proclaiming love for her.
(Always Be My Maybe)

Breaking down in front of her friends and proclaiming love for her.
(Jerry Maguire)

Standing outside her house with speakers playing her favourite song.
(Say Anything, Easy A)

Serenading her in public.
(Top Gun, 10 Things I Hate About You, The Wedding Singer)

Climbing up her fire escape to hand her flowers.
(Pretty Woman)

Giving her a thousand flowers.
(Gilmore Girls)

Planting her a whole field full of flowers.
(Big Fish)

Going round an entire town trying a slipper on every woman's foot in order to find her.
(Cinderella)

Kidnapping her, keeping her in isolation and then, uh, gifting her a library.
(Beauty and the Beast)

Now, if she's already deeply in love with you, the Grand Gesture is great! Wow, look at his commitment! He did that for *me*? **LOOK HOW MUCH HE LOVES ME!** (Heart emojis till the end of time.)

But for someone you're trying to attract? The Grand Gesture looks – yup, it's our three old pals again – **forced, desperate and clingy.**

I'll give you an example. A female friend of mine was once being wooed (*love* that phrase) by a guy she mildly liked. She didn't fancy him *that* much, but he was OK. Then, on one of their first dates, he hands her an envelope. She opens it. Inside are two tickets to Disneyland Paris. She lives in Newcastle. The tickets are for that weekend. The subtext is: *you're coming on holiday with me and you don't really have a say in the matter.*

But it turns out **she did have a say in the matter**. They didn't go to Disneyland Paris. They didn't go on another date.

See ya!

If you're getting the impression she might not be *that* into you, don't love-bomb her with Disneyland tickets, endless bouquets of flowers and a suffocating affection. Instead communicate, talk to her, see how she feels and, if necessary, let her go.

Someone else will be around the corner who gets you, who loves you.

It just isn't her.

***

Even on an initial approach, when a girl thinks you're being *a bit much*, you must remember that she isn't in your head. She doesn't know what you're thinking or what your intentions are. *You* know these things, and might assume *she* knows them, but she isn't privy to your rich inner life, your entire history and your previous patterns of (let's presume) good behaviour. **She knows none of this.** She's making decisions about you based on very little information – what you say, how you say it, tone, body language – but it's the information she must go on.

Let's put ourselves in her shoes again, with the knowledge that women and girls are having to consider their safety so much of the time. **They have to make quick judgements and quick decisions.** Once you see that, you can understand how being too full on from the outset can actually feel threatening, even if you never intended it to seem that way.

Women have a very finely tuned sense of danger around men – even men they might know – and for good reason. So that casual comment you thought was funny? It might remind her of a previous time when a guy said something like that, and he turned out to be a *total dickhead*. That look you're giving, which you might think is sexy or intriguing? She might just think it's weird in that context.

SO MUCH IS ABOUT CONTEXT. AT ALL TIMES:

READ THE ROOM.

That sexy look might be perfect mid-kiss, with someone who clearly likes you. But maybe not with someone who's still making their mind up about you, standing with you in a chip-shop queue. Like, mate, you are buying chips, a situation that doesn't warrant a 'sexy' or 'intriguing' look, so, y'know,

'Why is he giving me that *look* here?'

What sometimes happens next (and I know, because I've been there plenty of times) is that you blame *her* for the conversation turning sour. '*She* made it awkward by reacting like that. *I* like me, and if *she* doesn't like me, what does that say about *her*? Urgh!' You were just trying to be nice/friendly/attentive, there was no need for *that* reaction.

Recognise that emotion? Good, cos recognition is the first step towards change. Put yourself in her shoes, and see if you can view things a little differently.

***

I'd quite understand if at this point you are like, **'Dude, this is all small stuff. Petty stuff. This is what you're picking guys up on?'** And fair enough, these things in and of themselves may be small, but they allow for escalation to that bigger picture we talked about earlier, where boundaries are overstepped. **None of it is trivial, really.** If we can get the small stuff right, then the bigger picture takes care of itself, which would mean no need for books like this talking your ear off about it.

Writing this book is as difficult for me as reading a lot of it probably is to you. It's forcing me to confront mistakes in my own attitudes and behaviour around women in the past. But we must always keep trying to better our natures,[9] or we'll lose ourselves to bitterness, blame and misogyny – the term for the hatred of women – and these are very destructive feelings on which to try to base a future. If she's saying no, avoiding you or ghosting you, then clearly she *just doesn't fancy you*. And *that's* OK. **You don't have the right to anyone's attention.**

***

Accept it, move on, and open yourself up to better and healthier relationships.

---

[9] There's that superhero theme again.

But I'm aware that doing this takes work and self-reflection, an effort that will often make the quick, gluttonous fix of internet pornography more attractive.

Hoooo, boy. Here we go.

WHAT YOU CAN DO

Good flirting
You are . . .

Matching each other in banter. There should be laughter in both directions.

Talking for an equal amount of time, instead of one person dominating the conversation.

Telling interesting stories and listening to her stories.[10]

Reading her responses to see if she is reacting positively to your chat and to your presence:

---

[10] Do NOT tell THAT story. You know the one I mean. Yes, you do.

- Is she smiling?
- Is she saying things to try and impress you?
- Is she maintaining eye contact?
- Is she keeping the conversation going?

If the answer to any of these things is no, then you might be in the realm of . . .

Baaaaad flirting
This might include . . .

Having unreasonable expectations that this encounter MUST turn into something more, instead of it just being a fun, enjoyable conversation in its own right. (Don't force it if it's not happening.)

Her looking around or over your shoulder or at her phone. That's a sign that she's hoping for an exit from the conversation.[11]

Finding that you're talking too much or desperately trying to think of something that will fill awkward silences. (I'll let you off a bit here, though – this isn't always down to bad flirting. Sometimes the connection and chemistry just isn't there between the two of you, and that's OK.)

---

[11] You told THAT story, didn't you? I tried to warn you!

CHAPTER 2
PORN ON THE ROCKS

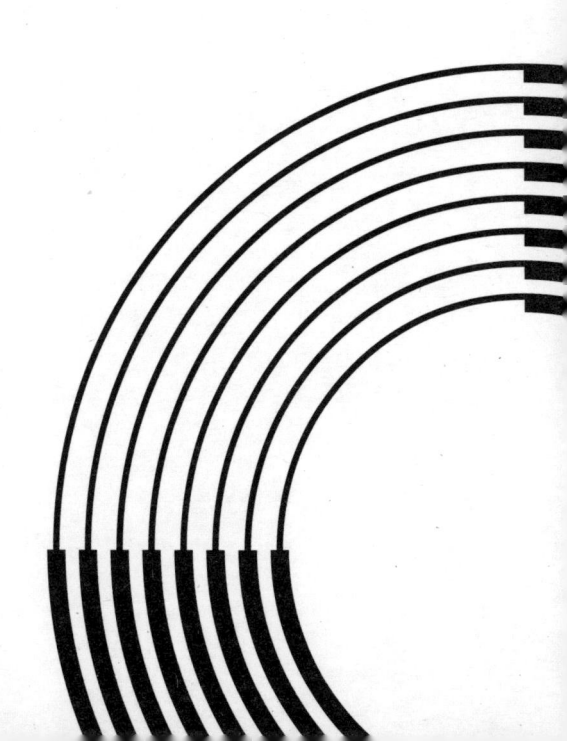

I would be as well just saying it: pretty much everyone masturbates.

Not everyone wants to talk about it, **but everyone does it**.

And why wouldn't they do it? It's great! It's You Time. It has a 'happy ending'.

And you can think about whatever or whoever you want when you're doing it, **because it's all in your head**.

And, of course, people sometimes want, um, visual aids to a good session. It would be difficult not to admit that the sight of gorgeous people naked isn't the worst thing in the world. I get it.

> **But internet porn cannot be the answer every time that need calls.**

I'm sure not *everyone* agrees about this, but most people would say: porn is not good for you and is far too readily available. In fact, in a recent study of eleven to sixteen year olds, carried out by the National Society for the Prevention of Cruelty to Children (NSPCC), 94% admitted they had been exposed to pornography and **10% feared they were already addicted.**

WHY DOES THIS MATTER?

Well, porn can negatively influence how you think about sex and relationships, it can leave you confused and worried, and studies show that not only is it addictive but it can also make you less respectful of women. And yet porn is eeeeeeverywhere.

I'm not going to lie, I've seen my fair share of it, but I honestly wish I could have those hours back, because I don't think I've got much to show for it, given the time I, uh, *invested*. These days, to make sure I get things *done* of an afternoon and be more time-efficient, as well as, y'know, not having a head full of porn, **I use internet blockers**.

I don't miss watching it.

Well, I do sometimes.

But not often.

Pornography, to quote the novelist Jeanette Winterson, is a **'highly toxic, addictive substance'**, one which has exploded in a massive way since the advent of the internet, opening a **Pandora's box of smut.**

So how did we get here?

***

Before the internet, if you wanted to communicate with someone who didn't live near you then you had to write them a letter or phone them. The letter would take days to reach them, and they would take days to reply. Phoning them sometimes meant waiting in a queue for a public phone box that smelled of pee, wishing the person already in it would hurry up and finish their call. If you wanted to 'share' a photo, you had to carry it to where another person lived and hold it in front of their face.

A lot of things were just a lot less convenient. **The internet has made them much, much easier.**

But it has also turned us into addicts. You'll have noticed it yourself: you're with your family in a restaurant and look over to see another family at the next table, or a couple on a date, or a group of friends, **all ignoring each other, lost in their phones**.

We've gained something and we've lost something. The world back then had problems that the internet has now solved, but we were more *present* in that world with each other. There was only one reality to inhabit.

And one of the 'realities' (or rather, **'unrealities'**) that we inhabit a lot more these days is that of pornography.

Before the internet, porn certainly existed, but it was very difficult to find. Some boy from your school would have uncovered a magazine left in the woods, and all the other boys would have been summoned to look at it drying out on a log, the pages all crinkly and rippled. Or someone would have located one of their dad's videos, a 'blue movie', and put on a secret viewing. **Porn existed at the margins of things, barely glimpsed.** If you wanted to go out of your way to see it, you had to walk into a newsagent – the same place people bought their newspaper, morning rolls and milk – take a magazine to the counter, then hand it to another human (often a woman) who would silently bag it and take your cash, in one of the **most awkward encounters imaginable**.

Even then, what was *in* porn was, by today's standards, relatively tame. Magazines featured naked women. Videos were men and women having fairly straightforward sex. **That was pretty much it.**

Now, however, people have instant, free, anonymous access

to a gargantuan library of every kind of porn imaginable, some of which is extreme, on the phones they take with them everywhere they go.

You can access porn as easily as you can turn on a tap (*easier*, even, cos who carries a tap about in their pocket?).

A recent report by YouGov suggests that around a third of men watch pornography at least once a week, including 13% who watch porn every day or most days. That is a change of enormous proportions from the pre-internet age. Our society is still trying to process the sheer amount of naked flesh to which it now bears witness.

What's it doing to our mental health?

What's it doing to our self-esteem?

What's it doing to our attitudes?

What's it doing to women?

What's it doing to men?

Internet pornography is a fairly recent phenomenon. We've only just started asking these questions, but studies show it's not looking great.

I'm aware that this is a discussion you might not want to have and, honestly, I'm finding this chapter a bit icky as well. **But we'll push on, cos it's important.**

You might be a user of pornography already, who is starting to feel a little accused, or even shamed by the line I'm taking here. That's understandable. And I'm not saying that all porn is 100% bad – fair enough, *some* of it is quite exciting and erotic and might seem to show people being treated with respect and, uh, let's say *positive attention*. But it can be harmful – to yourself and to girls too – **so let's dig a little deeper . . .**

1. IT'S ADDICTIVE

Porn sites, just like social media, are designed to be addictive, to keep you coming back, stoking up a craving that can never truly be sated. *It's not your fault.* They *want* you to lose hours and hours of your life on there. It gives them more hits and more ad revenue. That's why they always recommend more videos like the one you just watched, the algorithm learning your preferences and keeping you hooked.

There's always going to be a hotter video somewhere, right? And in the endless search for it, your brain starts to become *dependent* upon it. In 2014, a psychiatry paper was published with a title so long I won't even bore you with it, but which had the handy subtitle 'The Brain on Porn'. The findings suggested that porn can actually hijack the brain and alter its function. Your 'reptile brain', the primal, animal part, craves more dopamine – **the chemical responsible for pleasure** – so you keep chasing that next hit. Meanwhile, the neural links in your brain, which make up your memories, thoughts, feelings and attitudes, are changing in response to what they are seeing, meaning that **pornography is literally making you into a different person the more you watch it**. Interestingly – and almost hilariously – this behaviour is not restricted to humans; a 2005 study found that male macaque monkeys gave up juice rewards to watch pictures of female monkeys' bottoms.

We are literally acting like monkeys when we watch porn.

Sexy, huh?

Another experiment, by Dr Valerie Voon at the University of Cambridge, showed not only that porn is addictive, but also that regular viewers crave more hardcore scenes the more they watch it. **What once satisfied them no longer does so**, and they search out ever-more extreme images and scenes. Where this leads is not somewhere you'd ever have wanted to go before you started watching porn.

Pornography dulls rather than heightens the senses, but it can also waste enormous chunks of your life. I realised I had a problem with porn when I found myself waking up, opening my laptop and **watching it for most of the day**.

After I'd racked up enough days like that, I started to wonder what I could have accomplished in that time. I could have done some exercise, read books, met up with friends, learned how to play a musical instrument. **I could have done constructive things that would have made me feel better**, not worse about myself, and those are opportunities I'll never get back now.

2. IT'S NOT REAL

It's normal to be wondering about sex and relationships, but if you're looking for accurate information about what sex is like, porn is the last place you're going to find it. **In truth, pornography bears very little relation to real-life sex**, unless it is sex that has been heavily influenced by pornography.

PORNOGRAPHY IS LIKE FAST FOOD: PROCESSED, FACTORY-MADE, WITH ALMOST NO NUTRITIONAL BENEFIT.

Real-life sex – or at least *good* real-life sex – is like a feast, **rich for the senses and heaven for everyone to enjoy**. Porn simply cannot recreate this.

The age of consent is sixteen and it exists for a reason: to stop young people rushing into sex – or watching videos of other people doing it – before they are ready. There's a lot of pressure on teenagers to get involved with sex early, partly because it might make them seem more 'grown up' to their peers and partly because they are naturally curious. **But there's really no rush.** I didn't lose my virginity until I was nineteen and honestly have no regrets about that, because it was with someone I cared about and it turned out to be a lovely experience. You'd be surprised by the amount of people who leave it that long, or longer.

Wouldn't you rather wait until it's with someone special, where you feel ready and secure, rather than doing it with some random or because you feel like you *should*?

If you want to learn about what sex really is, what it looks like and how to do it, don't go to porn. **There are actual books out there that will tell you much more about it**, if you can bring yourself to read them. There are websites offering reliable advice that you will find links to at the end of this book. You could even talk to girls you are close friends with, to ask what most girls like and don't like, if that's a conversation you are both able to have. Frankly, once you are ready, you are going to be hopeless at sex the first few times you do it – everyone is! – but learn and try, and just as it is with everything else, you'll find yourself improving gradually.

And remember, your aim should be to give rather than receive, to do things *for* her, not *to* her.

After all, isn't that what you're hoping for from her too? That way it becomes mutual pleasure and not just one person 'getting their rocks off'. **Loving sex, unlike 'porn' sex, feels spontaneous, surprising, imaginative and often playful.**

Sure, it's sometimes awkward. Sometimes you both laugh during it, or talk during it. Sometimes you have to explain to each other the kind of thing you like or want or fancy trying, and there's a conversation to be had about that. Sometimes you have to stop because, y'know, it's not really happening, but it's all still cool, so you just go back to chatting and hugging or watching the telly.

Sex is a wonderfully human thing, when men and women (or men and men, or women and women) feel uniquely and truly close to each other. Even if you are not in love with her, or she with you, the emotions you experience are still very satisfying and positive.

When you are ready, **just be in the moment with her**, instead of trying to act out a fake and potentially degrading fantasy that you've seen online.

Porn takes the human element out of sex

BUT

doesn't replace it with anything more valuable.

3. IT CAN GET REALLY DARK

Yep, not only is porn fake, but it can also send out extremely unhealthy and violent messages about women. In a recent report by the British Board of Film Classification, 41% of young people who knew about pornography agreed that watching it made people less respectful of the opposite sex.

Why? Well, because what you're looking at, repeatedly, is sending you a very seductive but very dangerous and untrue message: that women only exist for sex. Every woman in these films is totally up for it, always open for business. No woman ever says no to anything, and the kind of sex they like is often rough and angry and painful.

Make no mistake, that's the message of most porn films that are targeted at men – which is most porn films, given men consume far more of it than women. This kind of imagery taps into and feeds something dark, something that wants to see a woman humiliated and hurt, and to feel as though she is subject to a man's every cruel whim.

So, who would blame you if you started to assume that's what sex with women is actually like, or should be like? I mean, you can see the evidence with your own eyes. There it is on film!

BUT THESE PEOPLE ARE ACTING.

It's a performance for the benefit of the film's producer, who hired them, and its director, who is off-camera telling them what to do. If the actress doesn't perform convincingly she probably doesn't get paid, regardless of whether she's really enjoying it or not.

Pornography can often normalise things like choking, hitting and calling someone disgusting names as mere 'sex acts', and, mate, why would anyone even bring that awful, negative stuff into something so wonderful? It's because they're following a script set down by a producer whose first thought is profit and who needs this film to be extreme enough for it to stand out in the very crowded marketplace of online porn. This is where porn gets dangerous, **distorting our understanding of the difference between sexual pleasure and harm**.

Pornography can coarsen attitudes to women and take us further and further away from being able to truly empathise with them, with their minds, their emotions and their real, actual needs. It's not making anyone a better person, and it's certainly not going to make anyone a better lover.

***

What I really want to say at this point is, 'If you haven't started watching porn, don't start watching porn!' But I'm aware that this probably isn't realistic and might even feel a bit judgemental if you have already started. It's natural to want to look. I mean, I certainly did. Just notice when what you are seeing makes you feel a bit . . . well, *bad* about yourself. At least think about what type of porn you're watching and how it's portraying women. And also pay heed when you find yourself wanting to watch more and more and more of it. Like other addictive things, what brings you in at first is the thrill of it. Everything seems new and exciting and kind of dangerous in a fun way.

Just know where it can lead. If you do get to a stage where you feel like porn is taking over, then there are apps for your phone and your laptop that you can download to prevent you from accessing it. Once you can no longer watch it, you'll be amazed at how quickly you'll stop *wanting* to watch it. Your neural links will go back to normal and your lizard brain will stop craving that dopamine hit. **You'll feel a sense of calm and relief, as well as being less depressed**, and you'll get more things done, with a renewed sense of purpose.

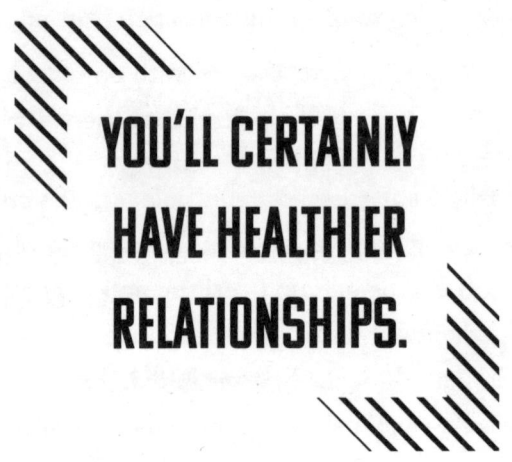

YOU'LL CERTAINLY HAVE HEALTHIER RELATIONSHIPS.

Also, bear in mind that if you do feel like you are getting addicted to internet porn, talk to a trusted adult or contact one of the helplines referenced at the end of this book.

They will understand and support you, so don't feel ashamed if you need outside help to stop. That's the brave part.

You can do this.

WHAT YOU CAN DO

How to spot if porn is taking over your life

- Is it the first thing you want to do as soon as you are alone?
- Are you anticipating being alone just so you can watch porn?
- Are you watching it for longer and longer periods of time?
- Are you staying up late at night to watch it, which means you are tired and listless the next day?
- Are you finding that you are constantly looking for something that's hotter than the last thing you saw?
- Do you find you are thinking about what you have seen long after you have finished watching it?
- Do you feel a sense of guilt or shame about what you have done after you've done it?
- Are you finding it's changing the way you think about girls, and not in a positive way?
- Are you losing interest in the things you used to enjoy?
- Are you putting off the things you should be doing because of it (like homework or studying)?

- Are you spending less time with friends and people who matter to you?

If you have said yes to any of the above, flick to page 190, where you will find resources and helplines. There's good help and information out there if you need it.

There is usually no one cause of addiction, and any addiction can be a sign that there are other things going on in your life that might require some intervention. Try talking to someone who you trust and who can help you get the right support.

CHAPTER 3
LOCKER ROOM TALK

I'm just going to put this out there: I don't think there's anything wrong with guys talking about how fanciable they find certain women.

There is absolutely nothing wrong with males enjoying female beauty, in the same way that women can enjoy male beauty, or indeed, **we can all enjoy everyone's beauty**!

I've been part of conversations with male friends, and sometimes female friends, about exactly which celebrities fit the bill of Most Attractive Woman in the World.[12] In an ideal scenario, who would you want to spend a consequence-free night with? It's a fun game that everyone can play, given that it exists in the realm of harmless fantasy.

UNTIL SOMEONE TAKES IT TOO FAR.

There he goes, acting out what he'd do to Taylor Swift, who just happens to have bumped into him in the local supermarket and has taken an immediate shine to him (even

---

[12] For the record, mine are Christina Hendricks in the TV show *Mad Men*, Bridget Fonda in the film *Jackie Brown* and Cybill Shepherd in the 1980s sitcom/detective series *Moonlighting*. OK, that's three women, but I can't pick just one.

though she's much taller and he's, y'know, *him*). And he's describing it in the coarsest possible detail.

We've all got a friend who takes it too far. Yup, here comes **That Guy** again!

It's a fact of life, but sometimes our friends argue with each other. Sometimes they'll argue about trivial things like football or brands of trainers, or which is better, an Xbox or a PlayStation, or whether or not Pink Floyd are the best band of all time.

AND SOMETIMES THEY'LL ARGUE ABOUT SOMETHING MUCH MORE IMPORTANT.

I once witnessed an argument between two male friends of mine which fell into the latter category, after one of them used the word 'it' to refer to a woman. This was a habit of his, usually reserved for women he found either extremely attractive or extremely unattractive, e.g. 'I would shag it,' or 'I wouldn't touch it.'

It.

Like, y'know, a chair or an elephant or Pennywise the clown. Not an actual human being.

My other friend had clearly had enough and questioned him on why he would talk about a woman in such a way when he had a sister.

'How would you feel,' he said, 'if a guy referred to your sister as an "it"?'

His reply was truly remarkable. 'I'm a big enough boy to know that's just how guys speak. As long as he didn't say it in front of me, then I'm none the wiser.'

Woah. SO much to unpack in that!

His first statement – 'that's just how guys speak' – is a variant on the concept of Locker Room Talk. This is a phrase describing the way men discuss women when no women are present. It was a defence used by former US President Donald Trump on the 2016 campaign trail, in response to a secretly recorded video of him boasting to other men about his approach to women. He said he liked to 'grab 'em by the p**sy'. The problem, according to Trump, was not what he'd said about women, but that a conversation which was supposed to be private had instead become public. *That was meant to be between the guys! And, c'mon, we're all grown-ups here. That's how men speak!*

My friend's defence ran along the same lines. *It's just Locker Room Talk.* He wasn't exonerating only himself but every other man who had described a woman as an 'it', an object, a *thing* to have sex with (or not, depending on what she looks like). By pointing out how *normal* it was, he absolved himself of any blame, in the same way that people avoid responsibility for toxic football chants if they're one of thousands singing them.

He further called upon the Trump Defence by stating that there was no problem with his sister being called an 'it' *if it wasn't said in front of him*, because, presumably, if a tree falls in the woods and no one is there to hear it, then it doesn't really make a sound.

But here's the real question we've got to ask: **if it isn't *that bad* to talk about his sister that way, then why would he mind if it was said in front of him?**

It's worth pointing out, of course, that we shouldn't need to have a female in the family to know that talking about them in this way is wrong. But for some men, **the harm only becomes real** when it concerns a woman that they *are* related to or care about.

Again, this might not seem like a very big deal, cos it's just guys talking, right? There's no actual damage being done, right? After all, no women are even present, so how can it be harming them? It all comes back to that sliding scale of behaviour we talked about in the introduction. The way we think and talk about girls and women affects the way we act around them. If guys are 'just putting it out there' in their conversations with each other and they don't get any pushback, they start to believe that what they are saying is acceptable and so could be more likely to 'push it' around women. This is why women don't tend to like it when they hear men – especially men they don't really know – being coarse or degrading in the way they talk about women: it's an indication that this man could be insensitive or even dangerous in his *actual dealings* with women.

So, it's not 'just' Locker Room Talk. And my mate knew that.

But also, *I* knew that. And I hadn't challenged him on it.

Because he was a mate.

There *is* a difference in the way lots of men talk when women are not in the room. There's a difference in the way these men talk *about* women. It's sometimes subtle, but it's there.

It's a bonding exercise. Like sitting round a fire, or going on a stag night, or competitive farting: talking about hot women can be one of the things heterosexual men do together. If it's respectful – y'know, kinda limited to a general appreciation of her beauty – **that's OK.** After all, when heterosexual women talk to each other, hot men can sometimes be a topic too.

But with some men, it comes with a sense of ownership and malice. So Donald Trump, a man who is so desperate to be an Alpha Male that he built a tower and named it after himself[13] and became, briefly, The Most Powerful Man in the World? *Of course* he boasts about grabbing women by the p**sy. Why *wouldn't* he? What is he, some sort of weak, limp-wristed, broke-ass loser? REAL MEN GRAB WOMEN BY THEIR GENITALS, GOD DAMN IT!

Or at least that's what he'd like you to believe.

---

[13] Phallic symbol alert!

WARNING

BEWARE THE ALPHA MALE, GENTS. BEWARE HIS STORIES.

WARNING

Listen to the conversations that men sometimes have about women and you'll find a similar jostling to impress, especially after they've scored with one and want to tell everyone about it. That's about boosting status. The more stereotypically 'masculine' the environment – male sports teams, for example, or gangs – the more hierarchical and competitive it is, the more common Locker Room Talk will be (I mean, there will be *actual lockers* present for some of these conversations). It's all dismissed or laughed off as 'banter', as mere social lubricant – just like alcohol, high-fives and comedy roastings of each other – as each guy attempts to prove to the group that they 'get it'.

'That's just how guys talk.'

Here we can include things like casual sexism, the sharing of stereotypes about women that some men like to indulge in.

Let's take some of the most common ones and break them down.

Women belong in the kitchen/the home. This stems from a time when, traditionally, women and men had much more rigidly defined social roles. Generally, men went out to work and women were often expected to stay at home and raise the kids. **We've come a long way since then**, and thankfully most of us now agree that men are capable child-rearers (ask any dedicated father) and that women are just as adept in the workplace. And in those households where a woman has chosen to stay at home, it's still a heroic task, since cleaning and tidying, running a household, stocking up on food and taking care of small children is exhausting and demanding labour.

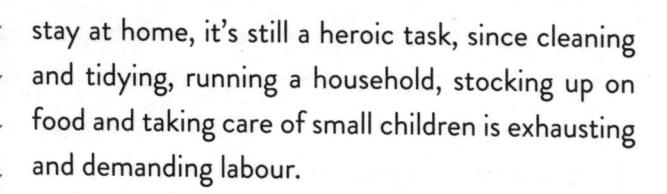

And can men not cook, or have I just imagined all those male celebrity chefs?

Women are too emotional. While it's true that women probably cry more than men, there are various chemical and hormonal reasons for that, plus thousands of years of culture wrongly telling men that showing emotion is unmanly. Unless it's for football reasons. Only then are they allowed to weep with joy, show that they feel broken by defeat, or kiss and hug other men. Indeed, men who *don't* expresss emotion when watching football are deemed suspicious by men who do.

But if a woman cries when watching a film or having an argument, it's annoying to those same men?

MWAP! MWAP!
◀◀ DOUBLE-STANDARD ALERT! ▶▶

Women are not good drivers. Studies show that men cause more traffic accidents, are more likely to engage in risky driving, are more likely to drive under the influence of alcohol and drugs, and are more likely to break the speed limit than women.

So, eh, no.

Women are obsessed with shopping and their looks. There is a ton of pressure on girls, from quite a young age, to look beautiful. Girls learn about make-up and dressing in fancy clothes very early. Just look at magazines, social media and newspaper articles. The culture in which we live suggests women are judged on the way they appear, in a way that men are not. Put it this way, if a man of any age is seen out in public without his hair done, looking a bit scruffy or wearing an old T-shirt, nobody bats an eyelid. If a woman is seen in public without make-up on or her hair done, people presume she's either old and past it or is having a nervous breakdown. As such, it's a very expensive, time-consuming business being a woman. **It's a whole production.** And there is an industry worth billions targeting them, telling them they're not good-looking or slim enough *yet*. They're judged on their shoes, skin, shape and hair, on how fashionable (or not) their clothes are and on how well they've done their make-up.

It's therefore not surprising that a lot of women seem obsessed with shopping and their looks. They're pressured by society **every single day** to feel that it matters more than anything else.

At the same time, there are a lot of women who would much rather dip themselves in sugar and throw a rock at a beehive than drag themselves round the shops every weekend, or who simply couldn't care less what people think of how they look. It's just that these aren't the women society often prioritises.

Either way, they shouldn't be getting judged for those decisions, and certainly not by men. Not given the way *we* dress, in our black/grey/brown/navy-blue uniforms.

***

As you can see, the basic stereotypes about women are flawed, and yet mocking them is a way for particularly sexist men to assert their superiority, for the benefit of other guys. All of it creates a culture in which men 'perform' at being masculine for other men – to be accepted by them, to be thought of as 'one of the lads' – using women as pawns.

And these men need to assert their superiority in this way because they feel either insecure or entitled – or both – which is what leads to them objectifying or belittling women, helping create a world in which women feel dismissed, unheard or unsafe.

That's what it comes down to, really.

***

In the TV comedy show *Key & Peele*, there's a great sketch in which two guys, each complaining to the other about their wives, have to check to make sure the women aren't listening before they drop the word 'bitch' into the conversation. By the end of the sketch, they are so desperate to impress each other but so worried about the women hearing them that they travel into space just so they can use the word 'bitch'.

We see similar behaviour online when male gurus set out to impress their legions of impressionable followers with ever-more outrageous or provocative statements about women.

Except they're not checking to see if the women are listening, because they don't give a damn what women think of them.

Take, for example, the former kickboxer and now internet sensation Andrew Tate, a jacked Alpha Male who poses with sports cars, guns and cigars. Before his accounts were deleted, he had millions of followers on Instagram and thousands of followers on YouTube. His TikTok videos have been viewed millions of times. According to a 2023 poll carried out by the charity Hope Not Hate, more young men in the UK have seen Tate's material than have heard of Rishi Sunak, the Prime Minister of the UK. He isn't some fringe voice randomly howling on the internet. He is mainstream.[14]

Andrew Tate says women belong in the home, can't drive very well and are a man's property. He says he prefers to date women aged eighteen to nineteen because he can 'make an imprint' on them. In video clips, he talks about hitting and choking women and stopping them from going out. In one clip, he acts out how he'd attack a woman if she accused him of cheating. In another, he claims that a man isn't 'cheating' if he still loves his partner while sleeping around, 'but if she even talks to a dude, it's cheating'. In yet another clip, he describes throwing a woman's things out of the window when he was upset with her.

---

[14] Though he did get publicly owned by nineteen-year-old climate activist Greta Thunberg, after Tate made a video boasting to her about his car emissions.

I mean, mate.

What?

Unfortunately, his influence on young men appears to be huge: a Hope Not Hate survey showed that 45% of sixteen to twenty-four year old males have a positive opinion of Tate (with just 26% having a negative opinion), some claiming that he 'wants men to be real men' or that 'he gives good advice'.

According to a 2022 report by Australian newspaper the *Herald Sun*, Tate is being blamed for a rise in misogynistic behaviour and attitudes in male private-school students, who swap what they call his 'Tate-isms' as part of their banter.

Presumably, given the stats, he's having a similar effect in schools that are not private, Australian or all male.

Right, let's unpack this. If this was a guy actually at your school or college, what would you think of him? Would you think he's cool and be desperate for his approval? Or would you think he's an arrogant tosser and want nothing to do with him?

Does it make a difference if he's online? It seems to. The internet creates enough distance that viewers can enjoy the 'edginess' of his opinions without any of the risks of actually knowing him in real life (where, let's face it, he'd probably be bullying everyone).

Obviously, there's an attraction to edgy humour. It makes you feel rebellious, free almost, as though you are throwing off the norms and rules laid down by parents, teachers and society. This frisson of excitement is greater when generated by someone successful or glamourous, whether a comedian on-stage with an audience of thousands or a pumped-up former kickboxer with millions of online followers. Plus, of course, there's safety in crowds. If someone can command that size of an audience, then you're not the only one getting off on this, right? He must be scratching a cultural itch, surely?

BUT IS HE SCRATCHING AN ITCH? OR CREATING AN ITCH TO BE SCRATCHED?

If you already feel that girls don't pay you enough attention, it's tempting to turn to a powerful man who 'puts them in their place', who re-asserts male dominance over women. It's a form of collective revenge, almost, and a way to feel justified about your negative feelings towards women.

But always think to yourself: **what is this man getting out of this?** What's the upside to *him* of your attention? Andrew Tate is a very successful man. He wants to generate followers, clicks, shares, likes, revenue. He knows that controversy and 'saying the unsayable' – especially in these supposedly woke times – is a surefire route to that.

These men are selling you not only lies about women but ones about men too: that being a true male involves being like *them*, a wealthy, ripped, tattooed, aggressive, dominant, arrogant Alpha dog who bites and doesn't care about the consequences.

But who on earth can live up to that every day of their life?

Could this be just a tiny wee bit *unrealistic*?

Is that maybe reducing masculinity to a *cartoon*?

And can believing in this cartoon be harmful to men?

In 2021, among men aged twenty to thirty-four, suicide was the leading cause of death in England and Wales.

What's going on with men? Could the pressures we are under contribute to our mental health issues and suicide risk? Could it be linked to what we are expected to *be* in this society, the impossible standards of 'masculinity' we are required to live up to, in which strength, selfishness and ruthlessness are rewarded and supposed 'weakness' is punished?

Where does this leave men who feel they don't have it in them to be hyper-masculine 'winners' all the time, who often feel sad or vulnerable, or that they don't fit in with the 'jocks'? Are we simply supposed to not express our feelings, or never cry when we are down, in case it somehow makes us look feminine? Might bottling up all this emotion actually make us *more* likely to self-destruct?

Maybe the people who care about us and let us talk about our more confusing or painful emotions are the ones we should truly value. Maybe that kind of communication and empathy is the mark of a good friendship, and of a good man.

A quick, **'HOW YOU DOING, MATE?'** can get us through some dark times in a way that tossing a woman's possessions out of the window in order to show her who's boss will not.

Make no mistake, Alpha Male behaviour is a sign of weakness, not of strength. Constantly having to prove to yourself and to other men that you're a player or the top dog is exhausting and desperate. Learning to feel comfortable in your own skin, not having to dominate others or brag about grabbing women by the p**sy – or describe in detail what you would do to 'it', given half the chance – leads not only to a more relaxed outlook on life but a more honest and genuine relationship with yourself and the world around you.

So when it comes to these supermen online gurus, always ask yourself: why are they never smiling? Why are they always frowning or grimacing? Why do they appear to be so full of anger? Why do they seem tense all the time? Why are their jokes always at someone else's expense? Is that the sort of man you think can teach you how to be happier? Would you *really* want to know this person in real life? Do you think he'd respect you in real life? Do you think there's the possibility that he would rip you apart in front of other people, for the benefit of making himself look good? These men think that because this is how *they* play the game, then it must be how everyone plays the game, because the game is there to be played.

But life is not a game. It's hard enough without trying to turn everyone into a chess piece to be moved.

Maybe the Alpha Males don't have our best interests at heart, and want to use *us* as pawns to boost themselves in front of other men, in the same way that they use women. And maybe if we simply don't give them that power – because, after all, they thrive *only* on the pursuit of power

– then they shrivel and die like vampires exposed to the sunlight.

Also, if they really knew the first thing about women, why is almost their entire audience male? Why do only 1% of females aged sixteen to seventeen have a positive opinion of Andrew Tate – **_1 per cent_,** as opposed to 45% of of sixteen to twenty-four year old males – **with 82% of females aged sixteen to seventeen having a negative opinion of him?** Does this man sound like *any* kind of authority on women at all?

Instead, women and girls follow men like Harry Styles: impish, talented, always smiling, *just happy to be there* and secure enough in his masculinity that he can wear traditionally 'female' clothes and people still find him hot.[15]

And when it comes to Locker Room Talk? Look, I get it. You want to learn more about girls, and chatting to your male friends about them is a probably a whole lot less awkward than doing so with actual girls or your parents.

But this learning should be an organic process that takes place over time, relying on being confident enough in yourself that you don't feel judged about your 'performance'

---

[15] Although I didn't really vibe with those 'granny pearls' he was sporting at one point.

or your masculinity, and can take it on the chin if you do mess things up with a girl **(which we all do).**

There's a difference between having a genuine conversation with a friend about how it went down last night and boasting about it. **Talk is good.** Putting pornographic ideas about girls you've been with into your mates' heads? **Less so.**

So in real life, if you do get lucky, and your male friends ask how far you got, give one simple reply, the very opposite of Locker Room Talk:

'A gentleman never tells.'

Not telling them makes you look cooler, means you don't have to admit that you didn't really have a clue what you were doing, plus the girl – and all her friends – will be impressed. **It's a win all round.**

But hey, what does this all have to do with you? Why am I even explaining this to you? You know all this, right? You'd never brag to the lads about the girls you've been with, or what you want to do to so-and-so and with her massive so-and-sos if you got the chance. You're not one of *those* brainless dolts!

YOU'RE
A
NICE GUY.

RIGHT...?

WHAT YOU CAN DO

Locker Room Talk

If you find guys in your company are being a bit too crude in the way they talk about women, there are things you can do to defuse it.

- A humorous but mocking comment – 'Do you realise how desperate you all sound?' or 'Guys who have to talk about it probably aren't doing it' – might be enough to call a halt without causing too much friction.
- Changing the subject to something you know they'll also enjoy talking about – whether it's music, movies, football or whatever – is another tension-free way of doing things.
- If it persists, then, 'All right, we get the picture,' or, 'OK, can we move on now?' is a signal that your patience might be nearing an end.
- If that doesn't put a stop to it, then maybe just exit the conversation; it will strongly signal your discomfort and give them the chance to consider that they might have gone too far.

CHAPTER 4
THE 'NICE' GUYS

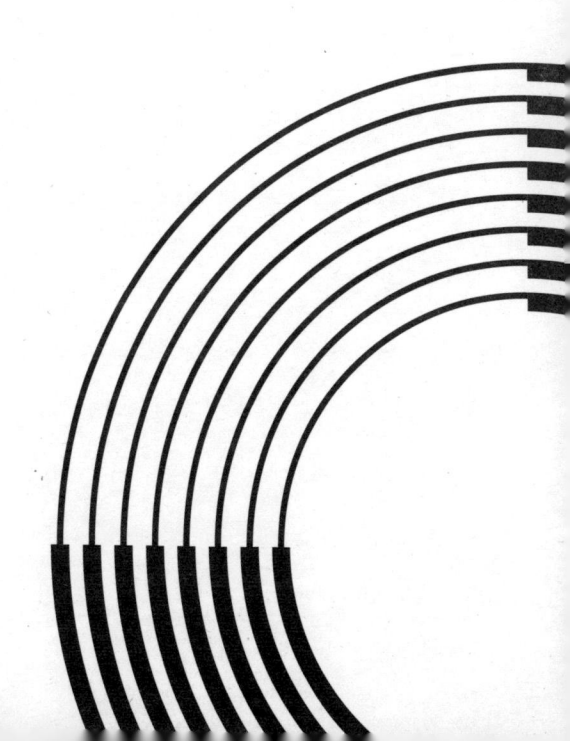

You've probably heard of the TV show *Friends*. Back in the nineties it was far and away one of the most popular TV shows on the planet, and at the centre of it was a will-they-won't-they relationship between two of the Friends: Rachel Green and Ross Geller.[16]

Ross was the archetypal Nice Guy. He didn't engage in the promiscuous 'how *you* doin'?' routines of Joey and wasn't full of self-loathing snark like Chandler. All he wanted was to be there for Rachel, the love of his life, whom he'd adored from afar since he was a geeky teenager and she was his little sister's best pal.

For all of season one, Ross hangs around waiting for Rachel in the Friend Zone (see what I did there?), till the moment in season two that everyone's been hoping for – Rachel realising her true feelings for Ross – and then they become an on-off couple for the rest of the show's ten seasons.

It's the triumph of the underdog, the patience of the sweet, sensitive, intelligent **Nice Guy** being rewarded, as one of the most beautiful women in the world finally becomes his.

> **For ever
> and ever
> and ever.**

---

[16] Spoiler alert: they will.

(CUE SCREECHY *PSYCHO* MUSIC)

Now that we can look back on *Friends* nearly thirty years later, it's obvious that Ross Geller, far from being a Nice Guy, was probably the most toxic male on the whole show.

I mean, you've possibly already spotted his **Wearing Her Down** approach to courtship, but here are just a few of his Worst Moments:

- He gets upset about his son playing with Barbie dolls.
- He is suspicious of Rachel's male nanny, *because he isn't female*, to the point where he makes Rachel fire him.
- He sends an embarrassing number of bouquets, cards and even a barber shop quartet to Rachel's workplace because he is paranoid about her fancying a co-worker.
(hello, Grand Romantic Gesture!).
- He is jealous of every other male in Rachel's orbit.
- He makes Rachel choose between him and her dream job in Paris.

That's just for starters. If you type **'Why I hate Ross Geller'** into Google, you'll find a pretty long list. He's the sort of man that proclaims, with self-righteous fury, **'Why doesn't she love me? I'm a NICE GUY!'** while being a perfect example of the opposite of one.

And he's the sort of man we're going to have to talk about sooner or later. Because it's not just the Alpha Males who are a problem.

>> 'Nice Guys' can also be THAT GUY. <<

***

This one is particularly painful for me, because I was very guilty of this as a teenager. I prided myself on not being one of the 'bad boys', those perennially smoking hard men who could down a lager while simultaneously pleasuring one of the many girls who'd draped themselves around him, and probably playing keepy-uppy at the same time.

URGH, WENT MY THOUGHTS,

WHY DO THE PRETTY GIRLS ALWAYS GO FOR SUCH IDIOTS?

JUST LOOK AT THESE MEATHEADS! WHAT'S SO WRONG WITH ME, HUH?

Just to properly set the scene, at the age of fifteen – my peak **Nice Guy** phase – I dressed head to toe in black. I wore a black leather jacket. My bedroom was all black. Cos black is *cool*. I wrote poetry about girls I fancied and the tortured emotions I felt when they didn't fancy me back. I sometimes even read these poems to them. I hated clubbing and dancing, which I thought were just for superficial show-offs. I was obviously a virgin because, really, *who on earth would*?

But hey, I was a **Nice Guy.** And that was all that mattered. At least to me.

The thing is, I did have female friends, but patterns would form every time. Being so needy for love, and feeling so freakishly unattractive, I would mistake the friendship for something more, write her a poem or a long letter exploring what was in my heart, or ask her out. **Then she would have to put some distance between us, because now it was no longer a friendship of equals** but something a bit stickier, to be awkwardly managed.

I would interpret this as rejection, and then throw myself all in to the next 'friendship' with a girl in the hope that it would turn into something more and banish the pain.

Here we see the dictionary definition of a vicious circle.

Like, no wonder I wore black.

Look, we all want to be loved. It's a basic human need. We are social animals, who gain our meaning only from our relationships with other humans. There's a film called *Into the Wild*, based on the true story of Christopher McCandless, a young man who decided to abandon everyone he knew, everything he owned and all the money he had, to try to survive on his own in the wilderness for the rest of his life. He died alone, emaciated and in agony, having accidentally eaten poisonous berries – realising that his life had been about the people in it all along, and that we aren't *meant* to be alone.

The dude went to extreme lengths, and it's a shame he had to die for it, but I'm glad he got there in the end.

The 1984 song 'How Soon Is Now?' by The Smiths encapsulates the world of the lonesome teenage male perfectly. Lead singer Morrissey wails about how upset he feels when he goes to nightclubs, stands on his own and leaves on his own, reminding us that he is human and needs to be loved, just like everyone else.

We can all relate,

right?

For me, though, the most revealing lyric is when Morrissey tells someone to shut their mouth when they point out that he's going about things the wrong way. I mean, it's not hard to imagine them sitting him down with a cup of tea and saying, 'Morrissey, mate, why go to a nightclub on your own? That just looks sad. And if you're gonna go to a club, then *dance*. **Don't just stand about like a big lump with a quiff.'**

In amongst all his self-pity there's an entitlement poking through. He goes to a nightclub – *on his own* – expecting everyone to find him immediately interesting just for being there? He tells people advising him against this to shut up. He says he's fed up waiting to be noticed. But, really, would *you* want to go out with him?[17]

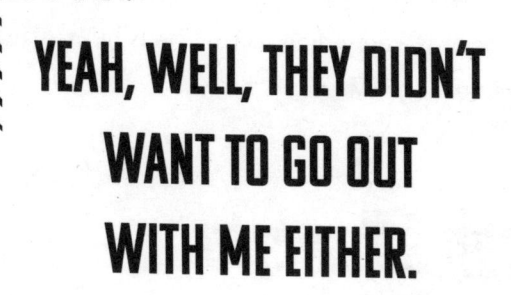

YEAH, WELL, THEY DIDN'T WANT TO GO OUT WITH ME EITHER.

---

[17] See also 'Creep' by Radiohead.

Perhaps if I'd accepted my female friendships for what they were – instead of trying to hurry them all into being my girlfriend – I wouldn't have felt so much like Morrissey in that song. Maybe by complaining all the time about how unattractive girls found me, I made myself unattractive.

Now look up the phrase 'self-fulfilling prophecy'.

What I did instead of trying to improve myself, and what self-described **Nice Guys** tend to do all the time, was blame the girls.

It's how, unbeknownst to us, while we are proclaiming ourselves **Nice Guys** – not like those dumb jocks, AS IF! – misogyny creeps in. This can happen even to the most sensitive of souls. We feel like we're owed female attention, and when we don't get it? It's as though we've been ripped off, as though women are denying us something that should be our right. We feel angry.

Nice Guys, the kind that I saw myself as, don't seem like part of the problem. They often go out of their way to be, on the surface at least, supportive friends, while secretly resenting that they are in the Friend Zone or not being considered as a romantic partner. They become jealous of the other men that she does choose, believing that *they*, the **Nice Guys**, are her true destiny, oh could she but see it!

Urgh, WOMEN!

All of this, however, is another form of male entitlement, because why does she need to consider you as anything other than a friend just because *you* want more?

Sometimes the Friend Zone is a lovely place to be, and **we should cherish being allowed into it**. There are upsides to platonic friendships with girls, the sort where neither person is trying to get into the other's pants. There is something wonderful about being considered a *genuinely* nice guy by women – someone they trust and want to confide in, someone they talk about in glowing terms to their female friends – rather than someone they worry about upsetting by not sleeping with them.

It's true that men mostly have male friends. They may *know* plenty of women, and of course they have female family members of their own, but would most straight men go to the cinema with a female friend, or even a bunch of them, or go for dinner with them, or even just hang out with them in their bedrooms one-on-one, *without hoping it turns into something more*?

True male-female platonic friendships aren't completely unknown, obviously, but they're a lot rarer than same-sex friendships. Boys, certainly from puberty, tend to hang out with boys because it's *easier*. It's less messy. Boys can talk to you about boy stuff.

BUT GIRLS CAN TALK TO YOU ABOUT GIRL STUFF. AND THAT'S CRUCIAL TOO.

The more time you spend with girls – especially when free of any romantic pressures – the more you *learn* about girls, how they think and feel, what's acceptable to them and what isn't. This becomes even more true when you spend time in and around *groups* of girls, seeing how they interact with each other. Because – *like this needs saying* – **all girls are different to each other, with varying opinions, tastes, personalities and rules**, then it stands to reason that the more of them you spend time with, the more you will absorb about the way they behave, the greater your sensitivity will become and the fewer silly mistakes you will make around them.

Being allowed into female company is a joy and a privilege for men.

Use it wisely, don't squander it and certainly don't go in there and make everyone feel uncomfortable by presuming, or even hoping, that they WANT you. **Go in humbly, with a decent bit of chat, and be willing to listen.** You'll find out a lot more about women from women than you will from other men – including me!

But also, read novels by women. Watch films written and directed by women. Listen to music made by women.

Most importantly, and I cannot stress this enough, *dance*. It actually staggers me how many men will react to an utter dancefloor BANGER with a curt shake of the head and the words 'I don't dance'. Women love a man who isn't afraid of dancing. It's not even about being an *incredible* dancer or anything, because who, apart from professional dancers, is? It's about just enjoying the movement and feeling free, with other people who are moving and feeling free. It's about inner confidence and letting go.

DON'T BE STANDING ON YOUR OWN IN A NIGHTCLUB, MATE.

***

As we discussed earlier, rejection can bring negative impulses out of men, which turn out to be very harmful to both men and women. We start to project our wounded feelings on to the figures responsible for our pain and ascribe negative personality traits to them. She must be superficial, or spoilt, or fickle, or manipulative, or evil. Maybe she's not the person you thought she was. Maybe she's turned out to be just like all the rest of them. Maybe there's no hope for you. Maybe all women are like this, deep down, just waiting to show their true colours, after they've tricked you into liking them, so they can hurt you again and again and again.

Thoughts like this are how the roots of misogyny can grow into a poisonous tree.

Shunning women entirely or thinking of them only as sexual partners – then feeling cheated when they don't live up to that – is a dark path.

From there, it's easy to exult in the macho posturing of the YouTuber who tells you that women need to be slapped around a little, or that they've rigged the system to keep men like yourself – **Nice Guys!** – down. You're open to easy answers, anything that will help your pain and confusion make more sense, anything that will stop you feeling less alone, anything that makes you feel that bit more like a king who should be able to have anything or anyone he wants . . .

AND THAT'S HOW MEN GO FROM BEING 'NICE' GUYS TO THE WORST GUYS.

CHAPTER 5
THE WORST GUYS

OK, this is the chapter you're going to enjoy the least. But it's also the one that's the most important not to skip. If you've stuck with the book this far, **you're doing brilliantly**. We've charted a course through some rough waters, and we're all going to end up sunning ourselves on the beach by the end and feeling good. But until then, there's one more giant wave to come – a tsunami, even.

SO HOLD ON TIGHT.

As the meme goes (kinda), let's look at how it starts, and how it goes.

Who are the Worst Guys?

What do they do?

This...

CAT-CALLING AND WOLF-WHISTLING

It's low-level, sure, given some of what's to come, and even if it's not being done to *actively harm* women, it sure as hell has the capacity to freak them out.

Imagine you're a girl (hopefully you've been doing a bit of that throughout this book, but it's a useful exercise anyway). You're walking down the street, on your way to the dentist or a barbecue or a meeting of the Trainspotters' Society of Great Britain. You're thinking about the day ahead or wondering where you can pick up something to eat or pondering what your friend meant when she sent that text without a kiss on the end of it. You pass by a group of guys. You notice them – of course you do – but not as much as they notice you. Then, from behind you: a long, slow wolf-whistle, a suggestive comment and a ripple of laughter.

What are your options?
a. Hurry away, hoping that's the end of it.
b. Shout, 'Thank you!'
c. Turn and confront them: point out how inappropriate wolf-whistling at a girl on the street is, running the risk that this encounter could turn nasty.
d. Immediately start kissing the wolf-whistler, hurrying him into a side street and ripping his clothes off – he must impregnate you immediately!

Most girls are going to choose a), because they know what wolf-whistling is: territory-marking. Even if this isn't conscious – what else can it be? No one doing this seriously thinks that's the way to win a date with the girl in question. It's letting her know that she is there to be *looked at*, regardless of whether she's going to a meeting of the Trainspotters' Society of Great Britain or not.

A few might choose b), but not many, since most don't want to encourage this kind of behaviour.

Even fewer will choose c), because they don't want to get their heads kicked in. Some will, through sheer anger, but there are definite risks attached.

Absolutely no woman will choose d), ever.

Like most of the acts on this list, wolf-whistling and cat-calling are about power. Even the metaphors 'wolf' and 'cat' suggest a power imbalance. It's not really about giving a compliment. It's about telling a woman, even a total stranger, that you can sexualise her at any moment, that you are sexualising her *now*, and there's nothing she can do about it. This can be incredibly intimidating and means women often don't feel safe walking alone. It's also a form of harassment, and a survey carried out by Plan International showed that nearly a fifth of girls and young women between fourteen and twenty-one have experienced it.

Cat-calling and wolf-whistling are a signal to other men that you are 'one of the lads' in much the same way that Locker Room Talk is.

A girl will **never** swoon into your arms after a wolf-whistle, unless she is already your girlfriend and has just come downstairs saying, 'How do you think I look in this dress?'

But doing it to a stranger? 'Hey, baby! Come over here, sweetheart. I got something to show ya! Oh yeah, I like the way you move that thing!'

You see how ugly it feels written down like that? Are you the sexy guy here?

OH, AND 'IT WAS A COMPLIMENT' IS *NOT* A DEFENCE.

CYBER-FLASHING

Don't send her a picture of your penis. Even if it's big and you are proud of it, don't send her a picture of your penis.

If she wants to see your penis, she will ask to see your penis.

At the very least, ask her if she wants to see your penis before you show her your penis.

If she says she doesn't want to see your penis, then *don't show her your penis*.

It's called cyber-flashing. It's sexual harassment. It's illegal.

IT IS, IN EVERY RESPECT, A DICK MOVE.

Up to now, we've looked at some sketchy behaviour: getting those romantic judgement calls spectacularly wrong; watching too much porn; talking about women as though they're objects, like household furniture; bemoaning the fact that they *just won't give it up to us*; cat-calling or sending them a photo of your junk.

All of this is very bad form, but much of it is not necessarily the result of men actually *trying* to harm. It's mainly a result of ignorance, clumsiness, naivety, inexperience or low self-esteem. Most guys who get it wrong aren't *setting out* to hurt women; they just don't know what they're doing and are caught up in a mix of thwarted purpose and confusion. Up until now, I've been thinking of them as someone who is trying to tie their shoelaces when drunk. **Though it should always be remembered that even if they don't mean harm, their actions can still lead to the sort of escalation that we discussed right at the start.**

But the very Worst Guys? **They know what they're doing.** They *are* trying to hurt. These are the guys that women are terrified of, and part of them *likes* eliciting that terror. It's the point of it. So, let's stare them in the face and see their behaviour for what it is, starting with . . .

REVENGE PORN

Revenge porn is when someone shares private, sexual content, such as photos or videos, of another person without their consent, to embarrass them or cause distress. This includes sharing online or with another person. It's called 'revenge porn' because it's associated with vengeful ex-boyfriends trying to get their own back – and it carries a possible jail sentence.

Look, if a girl you like has willingly sent you a picture of her naked, that's great. She obviously has the hots for you, and

I'm sure you'll enjoy seeing what she looks like without her clothes on. She might also want to see your penis! Go for it! Or, rather, ask her first, *and then if she says yes*, go for it!

THERE ARE SOME RULES TO THIS, HOWEVER.

Make sure she's not underage. Even if you are underage as well, technically you are now consuming child pornography, and nooooooo one wants that. You might also get a knock at the door from the police, or at least an angry parent. **Overall, you should both wait until you're at least eighteen before sending photos, however willing you both are.**[18]

---

[18] This is because in the UK, it is illegal to send naked selfies if you're under eighteen, even though sixteen is the age of consent for sex.

Faces aren't advisable, really. Not when everything else is on display. **And at least tell her that she looks fantastic. She deserves to hear that.**

BUT THE GOLDEN RULE IS

DO NOT SHARE HER PICTURES.

WITH ANYONE.

So don't share them with people she doesn't know you're sharing them with, and definitely not with people who know her. **That's not why she sent them to you.** I understand the bragging rights. You might want friends to know the level of uber-babe you're involved with.

Still don't share her pictures.

Or there might be a different motive at work: embarrassing her? What's going on there? If there's a part of you that *likes* the idea of betraying her trust, you need to explore the roots of that and address it, because that's some inner misogyny at work right there. It's to do with trying to make yourself more powerful by disempowering her, and no good guy should do that.

If you've been hurt by an ex or a break-up, there really are much more constructive ways to get past it: by talking it over with a friend, by simply learning from what went wrong and applying it to your future relationships. If you *really* want to get back at her in some way, then take a step back, focus on yourself and become your best self, so she'll realise one day what she's missed out on. But no guy can claim the moral high-ground after dooming a girl who once trusted them to a lifetime of potentially feeling shame, paranoia and even post-traumatic stress disorder – despite the fact that, to be clear, *she* hasn't done anything wrong – because her pictures might hang around on the internet for a long time.

If someone who has sent you naked pictures of themselves *ends* their relationship with you, for whatever reasons, delete those pictures immediately. **No good whatsoever can come from keeping them.**

WHAT YOU CAN DO

Let's be honest, most guys aren't going to confide that they've been uploading pictures of their ex to the internet, and if someone you know does, you need to remind him that this is a crime. If they're sharing naked pictures of her with you or their mates, you can also make it clear you disapprove.

- First of all, don't look: that might surprise him and make him stop and question his actions.
- If not, then say something like, 'Uh, does she know you're showing us this?'
- Ask him how he'd feel if she was sharing naked pictures of him for all her friends to have a good look or laugh at.

- If none of this works, then maybe a firm 'I don't want to be part of this' takes you out of it while making it clear to him that he's crossed a line.

INCELS

While we're on the subject of the internet, there are whole communities of men who huddle on message boards and around certain YouTube channels, and they are best avoided. You might sometimes hear them referred to as incels (involuntary celibates) or the Manosphere, and they tend to be men who feel disempowered and ignored, whether that's by women or society in general. The aforementioned Andrew Tate could be seen as the current king of the Manosphere, eagerly recruiting disenfranchised young men into the fold.

The Manosphere likes to talk about how duplicitous and evil women are – using derogatory words like 'cuck', 'beta', 'simp' or 'soy' for any man who happens to disagree with this assessment – and share videos of 'takedowns' of anyone they see as being against their kind, or in favour of women's rights.

'X DESTROYS DEMENTED FEMINIST!'

'Y RIPS APART BETA MALE!'

'Z DEVOURS BLUE-HAIRED SOCIAL-JUSTICE WARRIOR FOR BREAKFAST!'

Eesh! Overdoing it, much?

They are also exceptionally good at finding and recruiting young men online, and often start by pointing out how your favourite video games or movie franchises – *Star Wars*, Marvel, *Lord of the Rings*, *Doctor Who*, etc. – are being ruined by the 'woke agenda', i.e. people trying to make sure that women and other under-represented people are given an equal voice in our culture. You think, *Wait, that's right, the last few movies in that franchise have been garbage! Are they on to something?* You click on the video. There's an often highly entertaining man taking said franchise apart, laying the blame at the door of feminists (instead of just bad writing or poor direction), and before you know it you're being rolled by algorithms towards an online world in which there is no light and shade, no nuance, only endless bitterness and angry finger-pointing. *You are a man*, goes the message. *If your life is hard, it's the fault of the women who reject you and the feminists who hate you.*

No effort required on your behalf, and no need for men to take stock of their own behaviour. Just a very comforting and easy lie.

Become an incel by all means – it's as good a way at hiding from the more painful aspects of life as any – just don't ever expect it to make you happier or improve your relationships with women.

WHAT WILL IMPROVE YOUR RELATIONSHIPS WITH WOMEN IS **LISTENING TO WOMEN,** NOT TO THE MEN WHO ARE AFRAID OF THEM.

SPIKING

Oh, boy. I can't even imagine what possesses someone to put a chemical into a woman's drink or her veins that renders her incapacitated. I think we can all guess what the intention is. **But really?**

Spiking is becoming such a problem on the club scene that any woman will, as a matter of course, tell another woman to 'watch her drink' while she goes to the toilet, or will even take her drink with her. In a YouGov poll carried out for the *Independent* newspaper, a third of women said they knew of someone who'd had their drink spiked or that they themselves had.

THAT'S ONE IN *THREE.*

I mean, try to imagine going out with your friends to a party or a club – you, a male – and having to be careful that other men don't put something in your drink that will knock you unconscious, because otherwise you could find yourself waking up in a place you don't know and being sexually assaulted by them. **It doesn't bear thinking about, does it?**

Yet many women fear these things happening to them *every time they go out.*

Spiking, furthermore, is horribly easy to get away with. Less than 2% of reported incidents lead to someone being charged with the offence. People in a nightclub see a woman falling around and babbling incoherently and think she's drunk, right?

I mean, what sort of coward would do that to someone?

Sorry.

I can't even.

WHAT YOU CAN DO

- Always keep an eye out for your friends' drinks.
- Keep an eye out for the symptoms of spiking – these include suddenly **being sick, confused or disorientated, feeling sleepy, having trouble seeing properly, loss of balance, hallucinating or acting out of character.**
- If you spot someone spiking, report it to a member of staff or to an authority figure. Also, tell the person whose drink has been spiked *before they drink it.*
- If you are with someone who has been spiked, stay with them, make sure they get medical help and tell the police or an authority figure straight away.
- If you see a male friend spiking, then really, you need to end your friendship with him, cos that's a sociopath you've got hanging around you. You certainly need to, y'know, ***stop him from doing it***, even if that means reporting him to someone.

COERCIVE RELATIONSHIPS

Coercive control is when someone is being manipulated, psychologically harmed and prevented from living their own life by someone who is supposed to be their 'romantic' partner. It involves that partner having unfair rules for what is and isn't allowed, and they will often justify it by saying things like, 'This is for your own good' or, 'If you weren't like this, I wouldn't have to act this way' – putting the blame for the control on the person who is *being* controlled. Who wants to have someone knowing our every move, limiting what we can do and where we can go all the time? **It's a form of bullying**, basically, and it can be quite scary when someone wants to be in charge of shaping your whole reality and determining how you feel about yourself.

WHAT YOU CAN DO

Organisations such as Brook (sexual health and wellbeing experts) and Women's Aid give examples of coercive behaviour, whereby a boy or man is being too controlling with a female friend, girlfriend or wife. These examples include:
- Isolating her from friends and family
- Depriving her of basic needs, such as food and money

- Monitoring her time or finances
- Monitoring her messages
- Controlling all aspects of her everyday life, such as where she can go, who she can see, what she can wear and when she can sleep
- Depriving her of access to support services, including medical services
- Repeatedly putting her down or insulting her
- Humiliating, degrading or dehumanising her
- Subjecting her to threats or intimidation

If you think a friend or female family member could be involved in a coercive relationship, contact the National Domestic Abuse helpline for advice (or the equivalent organisation in your country), or encourage them to do so.

Make it clear you will be there for them if they do choose to leave their partner. This could be a scary moment for them, and they'll need to know they have support.

And here are a few pieces of advice **when it comes to your own relationships**:
- Never stop her going out with her friends or having interests that don't include you; if you feel threatened by that, you need to focus on

your own insecurities and why you feel that way, rather than preventing her from living her own life.
- If she is out, don't go texting or calling her every ten minutes, unless you think there are legitimate grounds for worrying about her safety. It's not necessary for you to know who she's with or what she's doing – if she needs you, she will call.
- Never criticise her looks or her weight, even if she is making negative comments about them herself. It's your job to build her confidence and make her feel good. After all, isn't that what you would want from her?
- In general, value her independence and unique spirit, instead of trying to shape her into something you want her to be.

It's worth pointing out that you yourself may face abuse or coercion from a partner. While far fewer women behave like this towards men than men do towards women, it is also not completely unknown and is of course equally unacceptable. **Support exists out there for men in such relationships, and you will find some websites at the back of this book that can help.**

We're nearly there, boys. The beach is in sight. Just a couple more grim things to look at, and then it's hammocks and cool drinks in coconut shells, I promise.

HARASSMENT

OK, so now on to something that is a very big umbrella term for many types of behaviour – harassment. Put simply, harassment is when a person repeatedly behaves in a way that is intended to cause the other person distress or alarm. This can happen to men or women, and can be conducted by men or women.

It's fair to say, however, that for all the reasons I've explained so far – not least the potential differences in strength and power – it's usually a much scarier prospect for a woman to be harassed by a man than it is for a man to be harassed by a woman.

The organisation Rights of Women lists examples of behaviours that, *when they are done more than once and are unwelcome*, constitute harassment:
- A text, voicemail, letter or email.
- A comment or threat.
- Standing outside someone's house or driving repeatedly past it.
- Damage to someone else's property.

- Maliciously and falsely reporting someone to the police when they have done nothing wrong.

Then there is sexual harassment, which is when someone inflicts unwanted sexual behaviour on another person in a way that will make them feel upset, intimidated, offended or humiliated. Again, this can happen to men or women, and can be conducted by men or women, but it is something women experience A LOT. **Don't believe me?** A recent UN study reported that 86% of woman aged eighteen to twenty-four in the UK had experienced sexual harassment in public places.

Eighty-six per cent!

It includes a range of actions, some of which are a criminal offence in the UK, such as stalking, indecent exposure and 'upskirting' (this is when the absolute worst of guys takes a photo under a girl's skirt or clothing).

Again, I'm sure you're reading this and thinking, *OK, I would never, ever do any of these things.* And that's good, I'm really pleased. But there are other examples of things that men often do, which might seem more low level, but which women have to put up with on a regular basis and can also be sexual harassment. They include:

- Sexual comments such as cat-calling and wolf-whistling, which we explored earlier.
- Making unwanted sexual advances, comments or innuendos, to make her feel uncomfortable.
- Bringing up sexual topics that she has made clear she doesn't want to discuss.
- Asking intimate questions she doesn't want to answer.
- Requesting nude pictures that she doesn't want to give.
- Sliding into her DMs uninvited and STAYING THERE.

You may think some of these could be fairly harmless, but as we've done throughout this book, put yourself in her shoes.

COULD THIS BEHAVIOUR MAKE HER FEEL ASHAMED? EMBARRASSED? HURT? OFFENDED? *UNSAFE?*

What about that last point, too? OK, there's nothing wrong *as such* with contacting a girl over social media or WhatsApp, although she's likely going to be rightfully suspicious if it's being done privately and there isn't an obvious motive like wanting to tell her about this jumper that you know she likes being in a sale at a shop near her right now, or updating her about the meeting of the Trainspotters' Society of Great Britain.[19]

A casual, 'Hey, how's it going?' to someone you don't know very well is probably a Red Flag straight away, but you never know, she might be up for the chat. If she isn't, she'll make it quite clear. You'll either get short, monosyllabic answers or she'll just ghost you entirely.

RESPECT THAT.

---

[19] No joke is still funny after the third time it's been made, so I'll leave it there.

WHAT YOU CAN DO

Helping women and girls feel safe in public

When nine in ten girls living in cities around the world feel unsafe, something needs to change. And even if you're not part of the problem, **you can still be part of the solution**. Here are just a few simple things you can do:

Part 1: If it's a pal

If you are with a group of guys and one of them is making remarks to a girl that are obviously unwelcome, then it reflects badly on all of you. So here are ways to deal with it:

- Something like, **'Mate, that's not even funny'** or, **'C'mon, just let her do her own thing'** are ways of letting him know that he doesn't have the support of the whole group. This doesn't have to be confrontational, either – after all, you're doing him a favour. You're his pal and you don't want him making an idiot of himself. A simple, **'Give it a rest'** is enough to undercut him, signal to him and the other guys that you're uncomfortable or he's embarrassing you all, which might be the

start of bringing them onside. It might even end up with the group laughing at him for it.
- If he's getting in her space, you can get in between him and her or start pulling him away. It will go some way to reassuring her that he can't actually get to her.
- Distract him: ask about something else or start a story about something that happened to you that day, and his attention might quickly wander from her.
- If he persists, then it might be time to be a bit more stern, something like, **'Mate, you're ruining the night'** or, **'Get a grip of yourself, FFS'** will mean he probably won't want to run the risk of annoying you further and might also make him realise just how inappropriate he is being. Whatever, he's less likely to do it next time.
- Unless he keeps doing it just to annoy you. In that case, you've got your own stuff to sort out as pals.

Part 2: If it's a stranger

If you see someone you don't know harassing a girl in public, there are a few ways to deal with it. You could:
- Tell him to leave her alone, but only if it's safe to do so – you might be dealing with quite a dangerous character.

- Otherwise, you can distract the perpetrator by asking him for directions or striking up a conversation with him; this will give his target the chance to move away, hopefully undetected.
- Ignore the perpetrator completely but ask his target if she wants to, for example, swap seats with you, so there's more distance between them, or pretend that you know her – this might be enough to put him off.
- Inform someone responsible for that public space, like a bus driver or police officer.

Part 3: Things YOU can do

There are also small things you can do, when you're out and about, that will help girls feel safer.

- **Don't stare:** OK, so she's sitting right opposite you. She's reading the book you like. But don't stare at her. Look at your phone or out of the window. Having a stranger stare at you is verrrrry uncomfortable. I mean, would YOU like a guy you don't know staring at you on the train or bus? No. Exactly.
- **Cross the road:** It's night time. You're on a street that is empty apart from you and a girl in front of you. Perhaps you're rushing home and she is in your way. Instead of walking closely behind her or pushing past her, cross the road. I know what

you're thinking: *Eh?!* But try to imagine you're a girl, and a guy you don't know is walking way too close for comfort, all the way home, breathing down your neck. It would feel threatening, even if it's not meant to be. Giving her space is just a good guy move.

- **This also goes if she's walking towards you on an empty or dark street.** You might not feel particularly in danger if a man is coming in the other direction – you're both just guys going about your business, right? – but I guarantee she will tense up a little until you are safely past her. Take that feeling away from her and just cross the street. Takes nothing out of your day, and relaxes her. Obviously check there isn't a giant articulated lorry barreling down the road before you cross it, though. Your safety is important too.
- **Don't run up from behind her:** Similar to the previous examples, if you're jogging, don't run right behind a girl. Again, it might be innocent to you, but it won't be to her. Hang back a bit. Let her get way ahead of you. That Personal Best Time isn't *that* important.

ASSAULT

OK, we're not talking about sexual assault yet, but that doesn't make it any less serious. Assault is when a person inflicts violence or makes someone think they are going to be attacked. Assault is never OK. Whether it's a man against a woman, or a woman against a man (or for that matter, a man against a man, or a woman against a woman), violence should never be the answer. But it is something we have to talk about here, because male violence against women is a big problem. In fact, **more than one in four women aged fifteen years and older** have suffered violence at the hands of their partners at least once since the age of fifteen. In the most extreme cases, this can result in death. A 2022 report from the United Nations detailed that over 81,000 women were murdered over the course of the previous year, globally, and that more than half (56%) were killed by their husband, partner or another relative.

To me, this is shocking. My own parents had a difficult marriage, which eventually ended, but there was certainly no violence. Not once did my father ever lift his hands to my mother, and I have followed his example into my adult life. I might have made all sorts of mistakes over the years in my relationships with women, but I've never made that one.

Unfortunately, some young men are given a very different example in their childhood, where violence against their mothers (or against themselves) may have been a feature. What these men take into their adulthood, then, can bode very badly for the women who encounter them, unless they take steps to deal with that hurt.

As with so many of the things we have looked at in this book, what seems outwardly to be a show of strength is in fact the opposite. Traumatised men often traumatise women. After all, men who are in control of themselves, who respect women or, indeed, humans overall, and are emotionally tuned in, barely need to raise their voices, let alone strike out with their fists. Men who haven't learned how to deal with an anger that may have had deep-rooted beginnings project it on to the people around them, whom they might have tagged as convenient scapegoats for why they feel the way they do.

Often, this means the wives or girlfriends in their lives.

Hitting a woman – any woman, but especially one a man professes to love – not only *won't* make him feel better, it will make everything in his life and mind much, much worse. He could seriously damage his partner, both physically and mentally, as well as destroy his relationship with her. He will have to live with the shame and guilt of what he has done, as well as the realisation that this is the sort of man he has become. **Violence takes someone far, far away from happiness and peace.**

There are support networks out there to deal with anger-management issues in men, some of which I've highlighted at the end of this book. But if you recognise yourself as someone who struggles with anger, there are small, simple things you can do to help control it:

- **Start with breathing exercises:** long, slow breaths that help clear the mind and bring your heartbeat under control.
- **Explore and practise techniques like meditation or mindfulness,** which can help to manage both emotions and anger triggers. These are used by all sorts of people who face high-pressure situations, from elite athletes to special forces soldiers or firefighters. It takes discipline, but if it works for them, it may well work for you. There are apps available out there that can help you meditate.
- **Channel your frustrations** into exercise that burns off your anger and clears your mind.
- **Most importantly, talk to someone** – whether it be a friend, a trusted adult or a mental health professional – to try to get to the roots of your rage.

Remember – one size doesn't fit all, but it is important to try out a range of approaches and see what works for you, and then practise doing it, especially when you notice the first signs of anger rising.

SEXUAL ASSAULT

Oh, god. It just gets darker, doesn't it?

This chapter is called ***THE WORST GUYS*** for a reason. In order to discuss the wound we need to look at the wound.

[HAMMOCKS AND COOL DRINKS, REMEMBER. WE'RE *NEARLY THERE*...]

Sexual assault is when someone touches another person in a sexual manner or makes them take part in a sexual activity *without their consent*. But sexual assault needn't necessarily mean rape. It can mean touching a woman somewhere she doesn't want to be touched, and you know the areas I mean. Grabbing a girl's bum on the dancefloor is sexual assault. Rubbing your crotch up against a woman on the subway is sexual assault.

A female friend of mine, who worked as a waitress when she was in her early twenties, told me once about a table of men she'd had to serve. They were drunk, loud and obnoxious. While she took their order, one of the men straight-up reached out, put his hand up her skirt and, well, did something that Donald Trump would be proud of.

They were thrown out of the restaurant, of course, but the police weren't called.

What sort of sheer arrogance and malice would you have to be filled with to think that was any way to behave towards any woman, let alone in a restaurant? Here we can see the 'performance' aspect of toxic male culture: is it likely that this man would have done this had he been dining alone? He wanted an audience. He wanted an audience of *men*. He wanted to put this young woman, who was only trying to help them have a good evening, firmly in her place before this appreciative, rowdy crowd, and so he did the most aggressive and possessive thing he could think of.

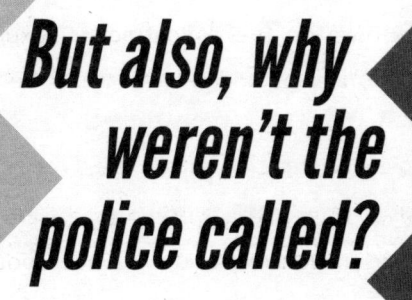

But also, why weren't the police called?

Had one of the male staff been assaulted by a male patron, would the police have been involved? Is it just something young women are supposed to expect as a hazard of the job?

And make no mistake, this is a male problem. Telling women that if only they didn't dress so provocatively, or didn't have so much to drink, or didn't make those kinds of eyes, or weren't, y'know, *being female right there in front of you*, isn't going to cut it. In fact, it's downright cheek. According to the charity Rape Crisis, 98% of sexual offences are committed by men. Proportionally, women *just don't commit sex crimes.*

IF WOMEN CAN CONTROL THEMSELVES, WHY CAN'T MEN?

Let's just keep our hands to ourselves. And if you have a friend coming out with that kind of patter – 'she was asking for it', 'she wants it', etc. – then something like a firm, **'Mate, that's brutal'** or questioning how he'd feel if someone was to say that about his sister or mother – even though, as we know, *it shouldn't take having a female relative for him to* *realise that women should be respected* – should be enough to put him in his place.

If it isn't, then I'd keep an eye on that one. Maybe even lend him this book after you've finished with it.

And if you think you've got the right cues from a girl, good for you. Just be mindful. You might go in for a kiss, and if she reciprocates, great. If she doesn't, then back off. We all get it wrong sometimes. But even if she's kissing you back, before you put your hands on *those* places, check in with her, and at least make sure she's happy for things to progress.

CONSENT, CONSENT, CONSENT, <u>ALWAYS.</u>

Speaking of which . . .

RAPE
There it is.

Well, we all know what this is, but for the avoidance of doubt, the Sexual Offences Act 2003 says that someone commits a rape if: 'They intentionally penetrate the vagina, anus or mouth or another person with their penis' and 'the other person does not consent'.

It's one of the ultimate weapons men use against women. I mean, I don't even like writing the word. I know reading it is enough to give you a heavy heart, and we're not even women. For women, it's probably one of the worst words they can hear, the worst thing imaginable.

Rape occurs with a depressing frequency. The highest ever number of rapes reported to police in the UK was 70,330, in the year ending March 2022. Bear in mind that five out of every six women who experience it don't report it to the police – either because they feel humiliated or because they don't think the police can help – **so the true figure is obviously much, much higher**.

Now, I know this is all feeling really grim and you might be wondering why I'm telling you this. I'm sure the very idea of rape sickens you, as it does me. You don't hold responsibility for any of those figures, so why am I getting on to you about them? Well, to do our part in making girls and women feel safe and heard, we need to understand why it is they often feel so unsafe and unheard in the first place. We need to acknowledge how large the problem is. And we need to understand why consent and respect are so important.

If a woman wants to have sex, it will be obvious. It is difficult to mistake the signs of arousal for something else. I'm not going to embarrass everyone by taking you through what they are, but at least one of them will be the word **'Yes'** when you ask that question you need to ask to know that sex is consensual.

The word **'No'** in pretty much any context surrounding sex is a refusal of sex, unless you have just asked, 'Do you want me to put my clothes back on and leave?'

Other than that, if she uses the word **'No'** then *for the love of god* stop whatever you are doing immediately. Read the situation clearly. Ask how she's feeling. Does she want you to stop this encounter completely, or does she just want you to stop that thing you are doing that might be annoying her? Seek *clarity*. **Clarity is everything.** Clarity, at this crucial moment, is what could stop her from being raped and you from facing a rape charge.

Even if she doesn't say no, then unless she actually says yes, *stop*. Silence is not a yes. Drunken mumbling is not a yes. If there is any doubt whatsoever that she might not even be *enjoying* it – even if her consent has been clear – then stop what you are doing. Ask her if she's enjoying it. If she isn't, then give it up.

The purpose of sex (and let's say here recreational sex, rather than sex where the sole purpose is to make someone pregnant) is mutual pleasure. If she isn't feeling pleasure, then there is no point in you just jackhammering away like a rabbit regardless.

IF SHE DOESN'T WANT IT, SHE DOESN'T WANT IT. END OF.

And, frankly, it doesn't matter if you think she's 'led you on'. It doesn't matter if she has been saying things all night like, 'We are going to have amazing sex later.' It doesn't matter if she's let you take all her clothes off and is fully aware of that thing currently standing right up in front of her. It doesn't even matter if you think this is unfair or that she's broken a promise you thought she'd made. There's no promise of sex that means someone can't change their mind about it later. It's not even up for debate.

If she changes her mind about having sex *at any point,* then that's the end of it. If you carry on, despite what she's telling you, then that is rape. There's no ambiguity to that.

If you are at all uncertain about the signals she's sending you, <u>ask.</u>

Because whatever 'signals' you believe a woman is sending out to the contrary, *no means no means no.*

WHAT YOU CAN DO

If someone tells you they've been sexually assaulted or raped, then the action required is clear.

- Call 999 (or your country's emergency services number) immediately: they may need both the police and an ambulance.
- Ask them if there is anyone else they want you to call.
- Stay with them; reassure them that they are now safe and that help is on the way.
- If they do not want to be around a man, then – with their permission – explain what has happened to a nearby woman or group of women: she/they will almost certainly want to intervene.
- If she is telling you about historical rape, then ask how/if she would like you to help. She may just want to unload about it, in which case be a good listener and *at no stage* ever suggest that she may have been at fault *in any way*. Point her towards the Rape Crisis helpline and even offer to ring them for her, if she would prefer that.

CHAPTER 6
THE GOOD GUYS

You did it!

You made it through to the final chapter!

I'm proud of you. I know some of that was dark, probably uncomfortable, maybe even painful, but you didn't give up. It would have been much easier to do that. No one likes feeling that they're being criticised – but really, someone who has made the effort to read this book all the way through, and listen to what it has to say, has proven that they themselves are **probably not the ones with the big problem**. That's not to say you can't still do a bit of work on yourself, of course: everyone will always still need to do that, me included, cos what are we all, holy men? But by even finishing this, you've already done a lot of that. **You certainly now know what the issues are.**

NO ONE CAN ACCUSE YOU OF SLACKING ON THIS, MATE.

There will be men who dismiss this book without even reading it, because they see the words **respect** and **consent** in the title, or because someone has taken a screenshot of a passage that *says something negative about men* and posted it online. As I mentioned at the start, some really will read this book only to attack it. Hopefully you're not one of them, but hey, if you are and you've reached *this bit,* then at least you've given me a fair hearing.

You might, on the other hand, be wondering *why* there are men out there who will bother trying to take this book down. It's very possible that you've read all the way through and seen the sense in it all. **Maybe you've come at it from a very positive place: you too want to be a better person or have a more constructive relationship with women.**

Alas, there are men – we talked about them in the last chapter – who not only think the problems described in this book are exaggerated (they say, 'well, there are women out there who MAKE UP accusations of rape!'), but also think that the women who point these problems out, and ask men to do better, are hatchet-faced feminists out to burn us all alive and that the men who support them are betraying their own sex because they can't handle life among the *real* men.

But they misunderstand the nature of strength.

You are not lesser for listening to women. You are not weaker for trying to learn how to be a more courteous and caring man.

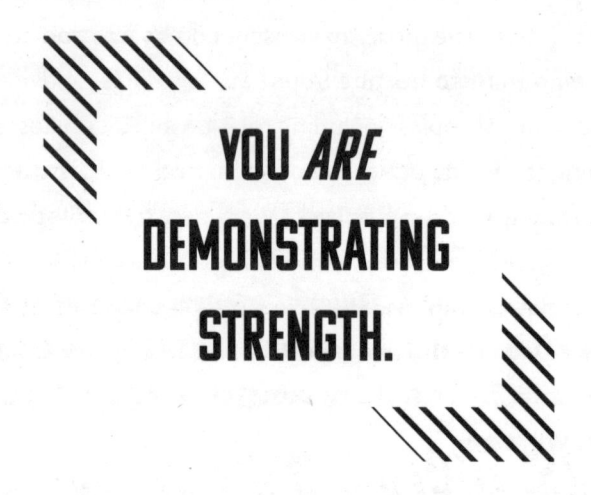

YOU *ARE* DEMONSTRATING STRENGTH.

It takes strength to try to find the sort of inner calm that means violence and anger are not your first port of call.

It takes strength to try to better yourself, to identify your flaws and work on them.

It takes strength to choose a different, less destructive path for yourself.

It takes strength to be a good man. A good person.

And there are other good men out there who will help you.

The Good Men Project is an online resource that aims to support males who want to be loving fathers, brothers, boyfriends, husbands and friends to women. It's designed as an antidote to the more toxic discussion boards and YouTube stars who want to nurture your hate, and offers advice on a broad range of topics, including relationships, families, sport, the environment, ethics, sex, health and wellness, and the soul. They even do movie and TV reviews. Examples of some of their articles include **'Three Things Not to Do When in a New Relationship'** and **'Insecure People Like to Put Other People Down with Their Words – and That's Not Cool'**.

Plus, there's a piece about Star Trek Day.

Beyond Equality (formerly known as The Good Lad Initiative) go into schools and universities to speak to young men about many of the issues that have been raised here.

Their managing director, Daniel Guinness, who was kind enough to speak to me as part of my research for this book, describes his aim on their website:

> There's a **need** and an **opportunity** in the UK to engage men in a **brave and transformative** rethinking of what **'being a man'** means for them and others.
>
> We need to engage all men in **preventing gender-based violence** and creating communities that are **safe for everyone.**
>
> We need to give all men and boys the chance to develop **identities** and **behaviours** that are **healthier for themselves and others.**

Also, Dan has great hair. Like, the best hair I have seen on a man since Michael Hutchence from INXS, who circa 1987 had **the best hair of all time.**[20]

---

[20] Just in case you haven't had enough references to the 1980s.

White Ribbon UK is a charity that aims to end men's violence against women, as part of the global White Ribbon movement. Their mission is for **'everyone, especially men and boys, to make the White Ribbon Promise to never use, excuse or remain silent about men's violence against women'**. They encourage all men to take responsibility and think about their own actions, in the same way that you have by reading this very book.

These organisations, and the men and women who work for them, are there to guide you through what might be very difficult terrain as you get older, should you need it. The aforementioned angry voices from the internet and the peer pressure to be *'ONE OF THE LADS'* will try to get their hooks into you. But I know that you want to grow into the sort of man that women feel relaxed, happy and safe around.

Compassion, fluidity, imagination, empathy, centredness, creativity.
These are attractive qualities to anyone – certainly to women – that are hard-won but ultimately make for a more stable mind, a healthier outlook on life and more enjoyable relationships.

Consider this bit the hammock on the beach.

Allow me to hand you your coconut shell, sir.

You've earned it.

***

In this book, I've tried to take you through some of the pitfalls of masculinity, the traps we fall into when we are trying to be a **'LAD'** and the consequences this can have for the girls and women in our lives.

We've looked at the perils of flirting, especially when we go 'all out' to try to impress a woman, failing to identify when she maybe just doesn't fancy us, and hoping to Wear Her Down instead. Beware the Grand Romantic Gesture, that over-the-top, throwing-everything-but-the-kitchen-sink approach that instead makes her feel suffocated and out of all proportion to your fantasies. And don't forget to keep your compliments simple, genuine and trained on aspects of her that don't have sexual connotations.

There's still no need to mention her earlobes!

We've looked at the dangers of internet pornography, its terrible, addictive power and the way it traps us in cycles of endlessly consuming exposed women, until our attitudes to them are coarsened by what we see and we start to think that, in real life, they want, need or deserve to be treated that way.

Porn is not real sex any more than pro-wrestling is real-life gladiatorial combat.

We've looked at the ways in which guys sometimes talk about women, to impress other guys, and how this has the effect of dehumanising them or turning them into objects of conquest.

Remember, a gentleman never tells.
Trust me, it'll drive your pals nuts.

We've looked at how rejection from women, or being relegated to the Friend Zone, can lead to a sense of self-righteousness from so-called **NICE GUYS**, which can curdle into a hatred of women.

DON'T BE ROSS GELLER FROM *FRIENDS*.

We've looked at how all these things can create a sense of entitlement or victimhood that make men believe they can treat women any damn way they please. Just like in the **Don't Be That Guy** script, these might be things that seem small and harmless, like wolf-whistling at a girl in the street, but when we let that happen and we don't call it out, it leads to a broader climate where women are objectified, with some men even harassing women for sex, swapping nude pictures of them with other men, spiking their drinks, hitting them – or worse, sexually assaulting them.

But we've also looked at how there are good guys out there encouraging young men to take a different path and supporting them on that journey.

I've talked a lot in this book about where men have been going wrong – me included! – but it possibly all feels a bit negative.

> So let's talk about the positive aspects of BEING A GUY, how important we are in the world and the good we can do.

We often hear, in our masculine culture, about the idea of men being 'protectors'. Now, we need to be careful what we mean by that, because some guys take it to mean being in a dominant or aggressive role, randomly thumping any guy that makes eye contact with their girlfriend. But, for me, being a 'protector' means
a girl knowing that

YOU HAVE HER BACK

if she needs you, and that

YOU WILL STICK UP FOR HER WHEN A SITUATION IS BEYOND HER CONTROL.

Your mates probably expect the same from you and vice-versa. Further down the line, you might take that role into fatherhood, which, believe me, will mean finding entire reservoirs of strength, patience, selflessness, empathy and, yes, protectiveness that you had no idea were inside you all along.

But they are inside you.

It's my belief that most men are basically good, but that we are subject to pressures – from society, from the internet, from other men who don't have our best interests at heart – which push us to be people who our better natures don't really want us to be. **Think about how you feel when you make someone smile**, or when you and another person demonstrate affection for each other, or when someone has been grateful to you for a kindness you have done them. And while it's not realistic to expect anyone to walk around just being 'nice' to everyone all the time (and as we know, we need to watch out for the self-proclaimed *'NICE GUYS'*), I do think the vast majority of men have it in them to be everyday heroes, avoiding the temptation to bully or dominate others, while trying to lift up people who might need it.

This book isn't just about being a better ally to women, it's about you becoming a happier person too. Even by reading this book, you've done a great thing and will hopefully want to make positive changes in your life.

You are not responsible for where society is and for all these awful things that have happened in the past, but you can help move things forward, by being a better friend (to men as well as to women), having stronger connections and showing understanding.

EQUALLY, WHEN YOU CALL OUT A MALE FRIEND, YOU DON'T HAVE TO DO IT IN A CONFRONTATIONAL WAY.

It's about opening up the conversation and stopping him doing something that might actually be pretty embarrassing, for him and for you.

YOU'RE DOING HIM A FAVOUR!

YOU'RE BEING A MATE!

WHAT YOU CAN DO

BE A GOOD GUY

- Listen to women and remember to make space for them to talk.
- Try to show you understand their perspective.
- Be on standby for when they need you.
- If in doubt, put yourself in her shoes. How do things look from her point of view? Could this mean an adjustment in your behaviour?
- Don't let your male friends off the hook when it comes to their own actions and speech, which might be damaging to women.
- Retain your sense of humour. Nobody loves a finger-wagging bore.
- If dancing is your thing, then DO IT! It can make a real difference to your mental health. If dancing isn't your thing, then at least try it. You never know; you might enjoy the feeling. If not, then that's OK. Good music on its own is always a solace anyway.
- Identify positive male role models, not only in your life, but in popular culture.

On that note, at the time of writing, the hero of the hour for fathers such as myself is Bandit, the dad in the children's TV programme *Bluey*. He's rare, as an animated father, for not being a total moron. Homer Simpson is a moron. Peter Griffin from *Family Guy* is a moron. Peppa Pig's dad is a moron.

Bandit is a cartoon dog with two cartoon dog daughters, Bluey and Bingo. He plays wonderful imaginative games with them that he's often just invented (to the point where he's maybe setting a wee bit of an unrealistically high bar for the rest of us). He loves his wife, he loves his daughters, he's a good laugh and he farts like a trouper.

What's not to like?

Maybe you've also been lucky enough to have a father or father figure who has been a good role model to you all your life. **If so, cherish him.**

If not, that's a tough one, mate.

But look around. Who are the older boys and grown men who do not make you afraid of men, who smile the most easily, who make you laugh, who bring a relaxed atmosphere to a room and whom both men and women seem to genuinely enjoy being around? **Study what they do and try to be more like them.**

I had a brief period, when I was thirteen, of playing in a local league football team. I did not enjoy it. The other boys were all set on becoming professional footballers, and their fathers would stand at the side of the pitch screaming with frustration at every missed pass or failed shot at goal.

Being a creative child, and only an average footballer, this was not an atmosphere I especially thrived in, and the other boys sensed it. Slowly, they started to turn on me, making it impossible for me to produce anything like good playing form, because my confidence was seizing up. This only made things worse, of course. Soon, the fathers started to join in with the name calling.

It's possible that I just didn't fit in that world, or that I wasn't a good enough footballer to survive in it. Probably if I'd been a spectacular player, things wouldn't have turned out like that. But I can only tell you how damaging it felt to be rounded on by the pack because they perceived me to be weak.

Shortly after that, I was 'adopted' by a group of older boys who lived on the same housing scheme as me. They were kind, funny and generous. **They treated me like a younger brother.** They introduced me to music and writers and movies that changed my life. I went through a troubled phase at fifteen – feeling freakishly out of place, as though I didn't belong anywhere – but they were probably the reason I survived it. Having a group of friends that I could talk to about these scary emotions is what saved me, in the end.

They called themselves

The Lads.

Thirty-two years later, our WhatsApp group is still called The Lads.

Now, all The Lads have partners. Some of The Lads have daughters. Despite all our faults, we have a vested interest in being good guys. We're imperfect, sure – and I'm not going to claim we fail to notice when women in movies we watch are beautiful – but crucially

WE TRY NOT TO BE DICKHEADS.

Up for that?

At the start of this book, I asked you what you thought a *'LAD'* was, cos it can go either way, really, can't it? Sometimes when we think of *'LADS'* we picture boorish drunks in town centres, swearing and spitting, fists in the air and a football chant on their lips. Or maybe we see a jack-the-lad, with an eye for the ladies, goosing a girl's bum on the dancefloor as though he's All That.

BUT A LAD CAN ALSO JUST BE ANOTHER NAME FOR A YOUNG MAN, A YOUNG MAN WHO COULD TURN OUT TO BE ANYTHING.

Lads can be a support group. Lads can be there for each other. A lad can be fun, full of banter, energy, enthusiasm, empathy and sensitivity, and still be, y'know, someone women – and men - want to have around.

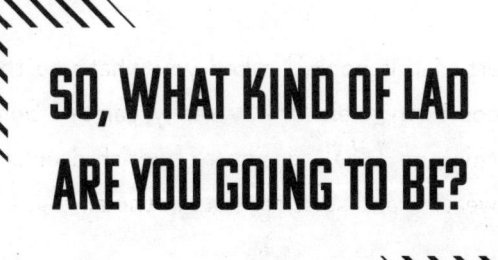

SO, WHAT KIND OF LAD ARE YOU GOING TO BE?

Now, as I promised, it's time for you to lie back on that hammock, enjoy the sun's rays on your face, and listen to the sound of the waves lapping against the shore. **You've done a good shift here, and it's time to kick back for now.** So what would you like to drink from that coconut shell?

Best of luck to you, mate, and thanks for listening.

RESOURCES

PORN ADDICTION
Sex Addicts Anonymous *saauk.info*
Provides support to help anyone who is struggling with addictive sexual behaviours, through anonymous and confidential meetings.

SEXUAL HEALTH ADVICE
NHS Young Persons Advice Guide *letstalkaboutit.nhs.uk/other-services/support-for-young-people/new-young-persons-advice-guide*
Online information hub and free, confidential, judgement-free sexual health services for young people.

Brook *brook.org.uk*
Offers sexual health and wellbeing support through clinical services, digital support, counselling and sex/relationship education.

Getting it on *gettingiton.org.uk/are-you-ready-to-have-sex*
Sexual and mental health information and services for young people, including advice on deciding when to have sex for the first time.

Health for Teens *healthforteens.co.uk/sexual-health*
Sexual health guides and advice for young people.

COERCIVE RELATIONSHIP ADVICE

Women's Aid *womensaid.org.uk*
National charity working to end domestic abuse against women and children by campaigning and providing frontline services and support.

Rights of Women *rightsofwomen.org.uk*
Charity working to help women by providing legal advice and information to help them use the law and understand their rights.

Men's Advice Line *mensadviceline.org.uk/male-victims/what-is-domestic-abuse/coercive-control*
Guide to understanding coercive control created by the team at Men's Advice Line, who offer support, practical advice and information to help men experiencing domestic abuse.

RAPE CHARITIES

Rape Crisis England and Wales *rapecrisis.org.uk*
Works to end sexual violence and abuse by providing information and support to those affected by rape, sexual assault and harassment, and all other forms of sexual violence and abuse, in England and Wales.

Rape Crisis Scotland *rapecrisisscotland.org.uk*
Works to end rape and sexual violence by raising awareness and advocating for justice, and to make sure that survivors can access specialist support.

The Survivors Trust *thesurvivorstrust.org*
Provides specialist rape and sexual abuse services in the UK, working with victims and survivors of all ages as well as their partners and family members.

MENTAL HEALTH CHARITIES

Mind *mind.org.uk*
Provides mental health advice and support, and campaigns to raise awareness and improve services.

Samaritans *samaritans.org*
Offers listening and support services over the phone or on email to people in need of help.

Mental Health Foundation *mentalhealth.org.uk*
Charity working towards a mentally healthy society for everyone by supporting communities, families and individuals through community programmes, research, campaigns and raising awareness through the annual Mental Health Awareness Week.

Young Minds *youngminds.org.uk*
Young Minds is the UK's leading charity fighting for children and young people's mental health.

Kooth *www.kooth.com*
Kooth is an online community for young people, which offers articles and discussion boards as well as online support and counselling over text and live chat.

Crisis Text Line *www.crisistextline.org*
A service that offers free, 24/7 mental health support via text message.

POSITIVE MASCULINITY ORGANISATIONS

White Ribbon UK *whiteribbon.org.uk*
Charity working to get men and boys involved in endling violence against women and girls, by building communities, holding policymakers accountable, campaigning for greater awareness and educating young people.

Beyond Equality *beyondequality.org*
Works with young boys and men to help them engage with creating safer communities, preventing gender-based violence and creating gender equality.

Good Men Project *goodmenproject.com*
Online hub sharing information and helping people participate in the conversations around masculinity and the way men's roles are changing in modern life.

REFERENCES

INTRODUCTION

'Statistics about rape, sexual assault and sexual abuse.' Rape Crisis England & Wales. https://rapecrisis.org.uk/get-informed/statistics-sexual-violence/, accessed 28 March 2023.

'Prevalence and reporting of sexual harassment in UK public spaces: A report by the APPG for UN Women.' https://www.unwomenuk.org/site/wp-content/uploads/2021/03/APPG-UN-Women_Sexual-Harassment-Report_2021.pdf, accessed 28 March 2023.

CHAPTER 2

Winterson, Jeannette. Quoted in Cunningham, Jennifer. 'What feminism means today.' The Herald, 31 March 2013. https://www.heraldscotland.com/life_style/arts_ents/13098308.feminism-means-today/, accessed 28 March 2023.

Kirk, Isabelle. 'How often do Britons watch porn?' YouGov, 1 July 2022. https://yougov.co.uk/topics/society/articles-reports/2022/07/01/how-often-do-britons-watch-porn, accessed 28 March 2023.

Kühn, Simone and Gallinat, Jürgen. 'Brain Structure And Functional Connectivity Associated With Pornography Consumption: The Brain On Porn.' JAMA Psychiatry. 2014;71(7):827–834. https://jamanetwork.com/journals/jamapsychiatry/fullarticle/1874574, accessed 28 March 2023.

Deaner RO, Khera AV, Platt ML. 'Monkeys pay per view: adaptive valuation of social images by rhesus macaques.' Curr Biol. 2005;15(6):543–548. https://pubmed.ncbi.nlm.nih.gov/15797023/, accessed 28 March 2023.

Voon V, Mole TB, Banca P, Porter L, Morris L, Mitchell S, et al. 'Neural Correlates of Sexual Cue Reactivity in Individuals with and without Compulsive Sexual Behaviours'. PLoS ONE. 2014;9(7): e102419. https://doi.org/10.1371/journal.pone.0102419, accessed 12 April 2023.

'Children see pornography as young as seven, news report finds.' BBFC, 26 September 2019. https://www.bbfc.co.uk/about-us/news/children-see-pornography-as-young-as-seven-new-report-finds, accessed 28 March 2023.

'"A lot of it is actually just abuse" – Young people and pornography.' Children's Commissioner, 31 January 2023. https://www.childrenscommissioner.gov.uk/resource/a-lot-of-it-is-actually-just-abuse-young-people-and-pornography/, accessed 28 March 2023.

CHAPTER 3

'Hope Not Hate profiles: Andrew Tate.' 31 January 2023. https://hopenothate.org.uk/andrew-tate/, accessed 28 March 2023.

Das, Shanti. 'Inside the violent, misogynistic world of TikTok's new star, Andrew Tate.' 6 August 2022. https://www.theguardian.com/technology/2022/aug/06/andrew-tate-violent-misogynistic-world-of-tiktok-new-star, accessed 24 April 2023.

'Suicides in England.' Samaritans. https://media.samaritans.org/documents/Suicide_Stats_England_2021.pdf, accessed 28 March 2023.

CHAPTER 5

Plan International. https://plan-international.org/, accessed 28 March 2023.

Our Streets Now. https://www.ourstreetsnow.org/, accessed 28 March 2023.

Millington, Hannah. 'Stella Creasy calls for "it was a compliment" to be dismissed as a defence for harassment.' 22 February 2023. Yahoo! News. https://nz.news.yahoo.com/stella-creasy-it-was-a-compliment-sexual-harassment-143139115.html, accessed 28 March 2023.

Oppenheim, Maya. 'One in nine women say they have had their drink spiked, poll finds.' Independent. 17 November 2021. https://www.independent.co.uk/news/uk/home-news/drink-spiking-women-police-b1956508.html, accessed 28 March 2023.

'Support for drink spiking.' The Mix. https://www.themix.org.uk/crime-and-safety/victims-of-crime/support-for-drink-spiking-44285.html, accessed 28 March 2023.

'Harassment and the law.' Rights of Women. https://rightsofwomen.org.uk/get-information/violence-against-women-and-international-law/harassment-and-the-law/#What%20is%20harassment?, accessed 28 March 2023.

Thomson, Rachel. '97% of young women have been sexually harassed, study finds.' Mashable, 10 March 2021. https://mashable.com/article/sexual-harassment-un-women-uk, accessed 31 March 2023.

Johnson, Sarah. 'Estimated 45,000 women and girls killed by family member in 2021, UN says.' 23 November 2022. https://www.theguardian.com/global-development/2022/nov/23/un-femicide-report-women-girls-data, accessed 28 March 2023.

'What is sexual harassment?' Rape Crisis England & Wales. https://rapecrisis.org.uk/get-informed/types-of-sexual-violence/what-is-sexual-harassment/, accessed 28 March 2023.

'Statistics about rape, sexual assault and sexual abuse.' Rape Crisis England & Wales. https://rapecrisis.org.uk/get-informed/statistics-sexual-violence/, accessed 28 March 2023.

'What is rape?' Rape Crisis England & Wales. https://rapecrisis.org.uk/get-informed/types-of-sexual-violence/what-is-rape/, accessed 28 March 2023.

'What the 32% jump in annual number of reported sexual offences really means.' Rape Crisis England & Wales, 21 July 2022. https://rapecrisis.org.uk/news/32-percent-jump-in-annual-number-of-reported-sexual-offences/, accessed 28 April 2023.

CHAPTER 6

'About us.' Beyond Equality. https://www.beyondequality.org/about/about-us, accessed 28 March 2023.

'About us.' White Ribbon. https://www.whiteribbon.org.uk/what-we-do, accessed 28 March 2023.

ACKNOWLEDGEMENTS

Thanks, first of all, to my editor at Wren & Rook, Laura Horsley, for approaching me with the idea for this book and for believing in it.

Thanks to my agent, Victoria Hobbes, for her encouragement and advice.

Thanks to Dan Guinness at Beyond Equality for his very helpful suggestions on previous drafts, and thanks to Paula Nagel for her feedback.

Thanks to Stand Design Agency for initially hiring me to work on their *Don't Be That Guy* video for Police Scotland, which ultimately led to this book. For the avoidance of any doubt about what my role on that project was, I helped them polish up their draft script.

Thanks to my sons, Fergus and Ivor, who make every day special and who give me hope for the future.

Thanks to all the women – especially my wife, Kirstin – who have taken time to talk to me about the themes of this book and where they think things are going wrong in our culture.

Thanks to my mum for being a great mum and my dad for being a great dad, the importance of which is only becoming apparent now that I'm an adult and a parent.

And to any women who feel that in the past I disrespected you, annoyed you or hurt your feelings: I apologise. It would have been through insensitivity, selfishness or emotional confusion, but it wouldn't have been something you deserved. And the fault was probably mine.

I'm still learning.

BIOGRAPHY

Alan Bissett is a novelist, playwright and performer from Falkirk, in Scotland. Formerly a secondary school teacher, bookshop assistant and university lecturer, Alan has been working as a full-time writer since 2007.

His first novel, *Boyracers* (2001) followed the formative years of four Falkirk teenagers, and his second novel, *The Incredible Adam Spark* (2005), told the story of Scotland's first superhero. His most recent novels, *Death of a Ladies' Man* (2009) and *Pack Men* (2011) were both shortlisted for the Scottish Arts Council Fiction of the Year awards.

He was Glenfiddich 'Spirit of Scotland' Writer of the Year in 2012, and in 2016 was awarded an Honorary Doctorate by Stirling University for his Outstanding Contribution to Scottish Culture.

Since 2011, Alan's focus has been on playwriting, and he has twice been shortlisted for Best New Play at the Critics' Awards for Theatre in Scotland.

In 2022, he was one of the writers of the Police Scotland video 'Don't Be That Guy', which looked at toxic male behaviours towards women and which went viral, garnering much praise and winning a PRCA Dare Award (for UK-wide PR campaigns) in the 'Public Sector' category.